AI YOUR FUTURE!

Dr. Koay Yin Yin

Copyright © 2024 by Dr. Koay Yin Yin

All rights reserved.

No part of this book may be reproduced, distributed, or transmitted in any form or by any means, including photocopying, recording, or other electronic or mechanical methods, without the prior written permission of the author, except in the case of brief quotations embodied in critical reviews and certain other non-commercial uses permitted by copyright law.

ISBN: 9798303245648

Disclaimer: The information presented in this book is for informational purposes only. The author and publisher assume no responsibility for errors or omissions or for damages resulting from the use of the information contained herein.

Table of Contents

Preface	5
About the Author	7
Chapter 1	10
Ride the AI Wave: Are You Ready?	10
Why AI is Revolutionizing Your Everyday Life?	12
Chapter 2	16
AI and Big Data	16
How Big Data Makes Everyday Life Effortless?	17
Unlocking Big Data: The Cost of Ignorance	19
Harness AI with Expert Insights	25
Chapter 3	28
AI's Evolution – From Vision to Everyday Impact	28
The Emergence of 1950s AI	29
AI: Exploration and Limits (1960s-1980s)	34
Neural Networks Reborn: 1980s-2000s	35
Deep Learning Boom: 2000s-2020s	37
Generative AI: 2020s & Beyond	40

Chapter 4 — 43

From Traditional AI to Generative AI — 43

- Traditional AI: Rule-Based Simplicity — 43
- Generative AI: Rise & Impact — 51
- Milestones in Generative AI Development — 55
- Generative AI vs. Traditional AI? — 57

Chapter 5 — 60

Generative AI: Shaping Smart Cities — 60

- Singapore: Innovating Services & Workforce — 62
- Amsterdam: AI for Sustainable Materials — 64
- Dallas: Enhance Self-Driving Trucks — 67
- Boston: The Urban Landscape — 69

Chapter 6 — 72

Generative AI: Redefining Global Business — 72

- Apple: Integration of Generative AI — 72
- Starbucks: Revolutionizing Business with AI — 74
- Mastercard: Personalization & Security — 77
- Morgan Stanley: Enhancing Financial Advisory — 77
- Allstate & BCG: Better Customer Experience — 78
- Goldman Sachs: Unified Power and Precision — 80

Klarna: Reinventing Shopping	81
Microsoft: Engagement Redefined with Copilot	83
Adobe: Enhancing Creative Tools	85
Salesforce: Redefining Customer Relations	87

Chapter 7 — 90

What is the Next Big Things After Generative AI? — 90

Predictive AI	91
Interactive AI	95
Autonomous AI	99
AI Your Future- Embrace the Transformation	102

Preface

What if you could transform complex data into actionable insights, make decisions with precision, and unlock new opportunities—all while saving time and boosting efficiency? This is the power of Artificial Intelligence (AI) combined with Big Data and Quantitative Finance, and this book is your gateway to mastering it.

With expertise in Applied Mathematics in Finance (Quantitative Finance), Big Data Modelling, and AI, I've spent years at the forefront of innovation, working with businesses and governments to harness these tools for transformative results. I've seen AI evolve from theoretical concepts to practical applications that drive profits, streamline operations, and create breakthroughs in industries.

This book distils my experience into a simple guide for anyone looking to leverage AI. Whether you're a business leader, a policymaker, or an aspiring innovator, you'll learn how to:

- Use AI to turn complex data into smarter decisions.
- Apply AI-driven strategies to cut costs and boost profits.

- Understand the key differences between Traditional AI and Generative AI—and choose what's right for your needs.

Inside, I'll share real-world examples from top companies and governments using AI to revolutionize their operations. From optimizing financial models to automating repetitive tasks, you'll discover how AI can be a game-changer in your field.

Welcome to a smarter, faster, and more innovative future. Let's build it together.

Dr. Koay

November, 2024

About the Author

Dr. Koay is a renowned expert in Artificial Intelligence (AI), Big Data, and Quantitative Finance. She holds a PhD in Applied Mathematics in Finance (Quantitative Finance) from Universiti Sains Malaysia and a Master of Applied Statistics from Universiti Putra Malaysia. With over 15 years of experience in education, data analysis, and consultation, she has a proven track record of transforming complex data into actionable insights that drive smarter decision-making.

As the Founder and CEO of DKAI Training and Consultancy, Dr. Koay empowers businesses, governments, and individuals to leverage AI for innovation and growth. She also serves as an AI Consultant for Timing and You Pte Ltd, a Singapore-based company, where her expertise has been instrumental in streamlining operations and improving efficiency. Her implementation of generative AI solutions has saved 50% of research time, enabled the design of a customized chatbot handling 70% of customer inquiries and cut 40% of the time spent on marketing campaigns—all while boosting profitability and reducing staffing costs.

Dr. Koay's exceptional ability to deliver impactful results is grounded in her robust academic foundation and professional certifications as an HRD Corp Accredited Trainer and a Certified Financial Planner (CFP®). These credentials further solidify her reputation for driving transformative solutions with credibility and expertise.

Globally acknowledged for her thought leadership, Dr. Koay has contributed to esteemed journals such as The Singapore Economic Review and the Malaysian Journal of Economic Studies. Her notable works, co-authored with Dr. Chee Wooi Hooy, include "The Role of Implicit Determinants in a Highly Liberalized Emerging Market: Evidence from Malaysia" (The Singapore Economic Review, 2022, vol. 67, issue 04, 1287-1305) and "Does Local Risk Still Matter in the Highly Liberalised Emerging Market of Malaysia?" (Malaysian Journal of Economic Studies, Vol. 60 No. 1: June 2023). These publications underscore her deep expertise in financial technologies and emerging markets, further solidifying her reputation as a leading voice in the field. Dr. Koay has presented her insights at esteemed conferences, including the 42nd and 46th Federation of ASEAN Economic Associations (FAEA) Conferences and the 20th Malaysian Finance Association Conference.

Dr. Koay's mission is simple yet profound: to make AI a practical tool that helps people save time, reduce costs, and generate wealth, fuelling growth and efficiency. Her vision is to empower individuals and businesses to harness AI effortlessly, unlocking potential and creating impactful, data-driven changes that enhance financial well-being and productivity. Her tagline, "AI Your Future!" encapsulates her passion for using AI to turn challenges into opportunities for growth.

To learn more about Dr. Koay's work or explore how AI can transform your future, visit drkoayai.com or connect via email at dkai@drkoayai.com.You may also scan the QR code to visit Dr. Koay`s website or follow Dr. Koay on social media:

Chapter 1

Ride the AI Wave: Are You Ready?

In today's fast-paced world, AI isn't just a luxury—it's the driving force behind transformation for businesses and governments alike. Fortune 500 companies are using AI to streamline operations and boost profits, while governments are tackling major issues in housing, transportation, and sustainability. AI has become the ultimate game-changer everyone's buzzing about.

Here's the challenge, though: while we're swimming in data, we often lack the tools to truly understand it. Every day, businesses and governments generate mountains of information, yet traditional AI struggles to unlock fast-evolving insights from complex sources like social media trends, open-ended survey responses, and product reviews. It's like holding a treasure chest without the key—so much potential, yet just out of reach.

This book takes you behind the scenes of some of the world's top organizations, revealing how they're using AI to solve real-world problems. You'll learn how leading brands streamline inventory, how forward-thinking nations optimize policy, and why the limits of traditional AI might be holding you back. More importantly, you'll see how Generative AI is completely rewriting the rules.

Packed with inspiring success stories and groundbreaking insights, this book highlights the next wave of transformation that's already unfolding. With Generative AI, organizations can tackle complex challenges and unleash AI's full potential like never before.

If you're feeling stuck in your AI journey or seeking a breakthrough, this book is your roadmap. Get ready to go beyond traditional AI, harness the power of Generative AI, and step confidently into a future of intelligent success.

"The pace of progress in artificial intelligence is incredibly fast. Unless you have direct experience with AI, you cannot imagine how fast it is growing. It's going to have a massive impact on the future of wealth creation."
— *Elon Musk, CEO of SpaceX and Tesla*

Why AI is Revolutionizing Your Everyday Life?

Picture this: You wake up in the morning, grab your phone, and ask your smart assistant for the weather forecast and today's news. Meanwhile, your coffee machine, connected to an app, has already brewed the perfect cup based on your preferences. That seamless experience? It's all powered by artificial intelligence (AI).

AI isn't just a futuristic concept anymore—it's a massive force shaping how we live and work. In 2024, the AI market is projected to reach an astonishing $184 billion, roughly the size of some entire national economies. And that's just the beginning. The AI market is set to explode, growing at an annual rate of 28.46% until 2030. By then, the AI industry will be worth a jaw-dropping $826.7 billion—that's bigger than the GDP of entire countries[1]! (Source: Statista)

---

[1]https://www.statista.com/outlook/tmo/artificialintelligence/worldwide#market-size

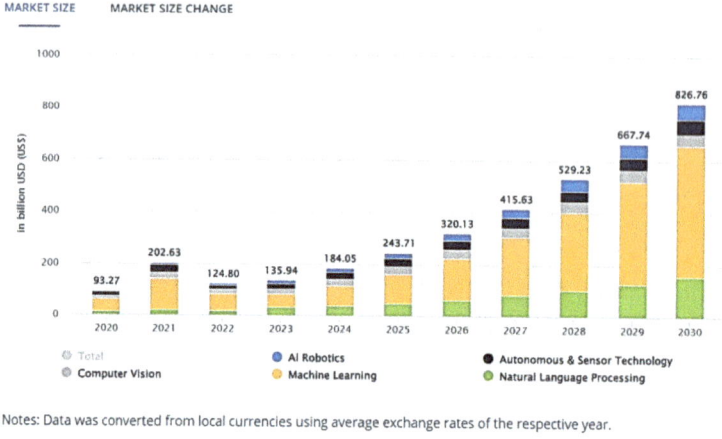

Figure 1: Artificial Intelligence - Worldwide
Source:https://www.statista.com/outlook/tmo/artificial-intelligence/worldwide#market-size

What does this mean for us? AI is now the engine driving everything from the way we shop, learn, and communicate to how businesses make decisions and governments plan for the future. It's not just for Silicon Valley tech giants anymore—AI is becoming a crucial tool in every aspect of life.

Take a moment to think about how AI helps us every day. When you open Netflix and see personalized movie recommendations—yep, that's AI at work. When you're shopping online and get suggestions for products you didn't even know you needed—yep, you guessed it, that's AI again.

Even when you're using your phone's facial recognition to unlock it—yep, that's AI.

It's not just about tech companies, AI is revolutionizing industries like healthcare, finance, retail, and education. Imagine being a small business owner running a bakery. You might wonder how many croissants to bake each day, what your busiest hours are, and how to keep your customers coming back. AI can analyse your sales data, predict customer trends, and even suggest when to roll out special promotions based on weather patterns or holiday seasons. It's like having a super-powered business assistant that never sleeps.

And AI isn't just making life easier for business owners—it's also helping governments run more efficiently. Imagine being in charge of city planning. With AI, you can analyse data on population growth, traffic patterns, and housing demands to make smarter decisions about where to build new roads, schools, or public housing. AI can predict where people are moving to, what services they'll need, and how to allocate resources efficiently. It's about making smarter, faster decisions to improve people's lives.

The future of AI is bright, and it's already reshaping how we experience the world. From our homes to our workplaces and even our city streets, AI is making everything run smoother, smarter, and faster. And as the technology continues to evolve, its impact will only grow.

So, whether you're running a business, working in government, or just a curious individual, AI is no longer a distant future. It's here, and it's here to help. In this book, we'll dive into how AI works, how it's changing our world, and—most importantly—how you can make the most of it.

"The key to economic growth is innovation, and AI is a critical component of that innovation. It's going to drive productivity and create wealth in ways we've never imagined."
— Satya Nadella, CEO of Microsoft

Chapter 2

AI and Big Data

Ever wonder how shopping, scrolling, or navigating feels so effortless? Behind the scenes, AI and big data are working magic, transforming the way we live by delivering smarter, more personalized experiences every day. Whether you're a consumer, a business leader, or a government official, this powerful combination is fine-tuning life's conveniences just for you.

Each day, our simple actions—posting on social media, browsing products, or mapping out our commute—generate vast amounts of data. This information flows from everywhere: your phone's location, shopping history, smart home devices, and even the temperature settings in your fridge. Alone, these details might seem trivial, but together, they create patterns that drive the insights shaping your day.

How Big Data Makes Everyday Life Effortless?

In ways you may not even realize, big data is at work making life easier, faster, and more personalized. From our daily commutes to the way we shop and even manage our homes, big data is the unseen force streamlining tasks and anticipating our needs. Here are some examples of how big data quietly works in the background, simplifying your everyday routines.

(i) **Navigation Apps That Know the Best Routes**
Ever wondered how your GPS always seems to know the fastest way to work? It's not magic—it's big data! Every time you open that app, it's analysing real-time traffic data from thousands of drivers, pinpointing congestion and clearing a smoother, faster route just for you. No more bumper-to-bumper surprises!

(ii) **Shopping Sites That Read Your Mind**
Ever wondered how your favourite online store always seems to know exactly what you're looking for? It's not just coincidence—it's the power of big data at work. By analysing your shopping patterns and comparing them with preferences of similar users, these platforms curate personalized recommendations tailored

specifically to you. The result? A seamless shopping experience that feels almost like the store truly knows you.

(iii) **Smart Home Devices That Think Ahead**
Your smart thermostat or fridge isn't just high-tech; it's designed to learn from your habits. It's big data in action, turning ordinary devices into helpful assistants that anticipate your needs. Your fridge might cool down during off-peak hours, keeping your food fresh and energy bills low—without you lifting a finger.

(iv) **Food Delivery Apps That Get Your Cravings**
When you open your food app, it knows your favourites right away. That's no coincidence. By analysing your order history and other users' preferences, big data helps the app suggest options you'll love. Rainy night? The app might even recommend warm drinks and comfort food, tailored to your cravings.

Big data is silently shaping the moments that make your life easier and more enjoyable. Every click, every choice adds to a web of insights that allow businesses and devices to meet you where you are. Welcome to a future where your experiences are tailored to you—one smart decision at a time.

Unlocking Big Data: The Cost of Ignorance

Big data may be quietly working in the background, making everyday tasks feel effortless, but what happens when we don't know how to harness its full potential? Despite the vast opportunities data offers, many businesses and individuals struggle to tap into this powerful resource effectively. Data is everywhere, constantly generated by our daily routines and interactions, but without the right skills and tools, it remains untapped—a missed opportunity with real costs.

In this section, we'll explore the common roadblocks that prevent big data from reaching its true value, and why overcoming these barriers is essential for unlocking insights that drive smarter decisions and real results:

(i) **Data complexity makes understanding difficult**

Imagine walking into your kitchen and seeing a table full of various ingredients—fresh tomatoes, onions, chicken, and spices. They're neatly arranged, suggesting that if you know how to cook, you can whip up a delicious dinner. But if you don't know how to cook, those ingredients are just a chaotic assortment of items. You know they have the potential to become a great dish, but you lack the skills to turn them into a meal.

The analogy of big data is quite similar. Data itself is like raw ingredients—vast and complex, often hard to grasp directly. It needs to be processed and analysed to become meaningful information. Without the relevant skills and experience, this data is just a collection of "materials," making it difficult to extract useful insights.

Real-Life Example: The Struggles of a Small Business Owner

Imagine you own a small store and have accumulated months of customer purchase records. These data are stored on your computer, and each time you open the file, you see detailed sales information—who bought what and when. You realize that there might be valuable insights hidden in this data, like which products are best-sellers and what times customers visit most. But since you don't have the skills to process and analyse this data, it appears to be "useless records" taking up space. You might wonder, "What good is this data? How can I derive useful information to help my business?"

This scenario is quite common. Many people recognize the importance of big data but fail to effectively utilize it due to a lack of expertise. If you could understand the story behind the data, you might uncover potential business opportunities and optimize your products and services. But without analytical skills, these data points are like disjointed puzzle pieces that fail to create a complete picture.

(ii) **Lack of Tools and Methods Turns Big Data into "Sleeping Treasure"**

Even with a strong grasp of big data's importance and access to rich datasets, without the right tools and analytical methods, the true potential of that data remains out of reach. Data analysis isn't just about looking at numbers—it requires specialized software and techniques to uncover valuable insights. When dealing with hundreds of thousands or even millions of data points, spotting patterns and trends goes beyond what our eyes alone can detect.

But tools alone aren't enough. Even if you have ample data and the right technology, without the knowledge of how to identify and interpret meaningful patterns, the data remains "dormant." Data itself doesn't hold value until we extract insights from it. Often, the real worth of data is hidden in subtle correlations that can easily be missed, leaving vast potential untapped.

Real-Life Example: Blind Spots in Running Data

Suppose you track your running data daily, including steps, heart rate, and calories burned. You have a clear goal: to improve your health. Looking at these numbers might be interesting, but if you don't know how to analyse them, you may not gain substantial benefits. However, if you can analyse this data, you might discover that your heart rate is most effective within a certain range, or that running during a specific time yields the best results. These patterns and trends are the most valuable treasures behind the data, guiding you on how to adjust your behaviour for better outcomes.

This situation is also common in business decisions. Many companies accumulate vast amounts of customer data and market information daily, but if they fail to uncover new patterns and opportunities, that data is just a series of meaningless numbers that don't provide any real value.

(iii) **Data Fail to Transformed into Action**

Even if you have analysed the data, if you don't know how to turn those results into actionable steps, the value of the data remains unrealized. Data analysis is not only about identifying problems or revealing trends; more importantly, it provides direction for action, helping you make better decisions. And this is the ultimate goal of big data.

Real-Life Example: A Restaurant Owner's Dilemma

Imagine you run a restaurant and have collected a month's worth of ordering data, detailing which dishes sell best and when customers visit most. However, you're unsure how to utilize this information. You might think that as long as you keep running things the same way, there's no need for adjustment. But if you understand how to leverage the results from data analysis, you might discover effective measures to take, like increasing the supply of popular dishes, launching limited-time promotions to attract more customers, or even optimizing staff allocation to improve operational efficiency.

If you don't know how to convert data into actionable strategies, the data will ultimately remain at the analysis stage, failing to have a real impact on your business. Those who understand data analysis can discover potential, make timely adjustments, and truly realize the value of data.

(iv) **Inadequate Data Security and Privacy Protection**

Beyond data analysis, managing big data responsibly demands a strong focus on data security and privacy. When these concerns are handled carelessly or without proper knowledge, the consequences can be severe. This is especially critical when working with sensitive customer information, where data security must be a top priority. Without robust security measures and privacy protections, big data efforts may backfire, not only failing to provide value but also leading to serious legal risks and damaging trust.

Real-Life Example: Data Hazards in an Insurance Company

Imagine you work for an insurance company and hold a wealth of customer health information and financial data. This data is vital for the company, helping assess risk and formulate policies. If you don't know how to protect this sensitive information, you might inadvertently store or transmit it insecurely, leading to data breaches. A single data leak can cause immense financial losses for the company and severely damage customer trust, possibly resulting in legal lawsuits. A data security expert would use encryption, access controls, and other measures to ensure that this information isn't illegally accessed or leaked.

"Without data, you're just another person with an opinion."
— W. Edwards Deming, Statistician and Quality Management Pioneer

Harness AI with Expert Insights

As we've seen, the power of AI is undeniable. From predicting market trends to answering complex questions, AI—especially Generative AI —can analyse vast amounts of information and provide intelligent insights. But to fully unlock this power, skilled professionals are essential to guide and optimize its use. Imagine AI as a high-performance race car: without a skilled driver, even the most powerful engine can't reach its potential.

Why do you need these experts? Here's how they help maximize AI's value:

(i) **Preparing Your Data:**
Before AI can unlock valuable insights, your data needs to be meticulously cleaned and organized. Just like a chef carefully preps ingredients before cooking, data preparation is essential. Errors, inconsistencies, or missing

elements can distort results, so starting with clean, accurate data is key to meaningful analysis.

(ii) **Customizing AI for Your Industry:**
Each industry has distinct needs, and a one-size-fits-all AI model won't address them all. By fine-tuning AI to match your specific business requirements, experts ensure that the insights AI provides are relevant, actionable, and tailored to your unique context.

(iii) **Turning Data into Actionable Insights:**
AI excels at processing vast amounts of data, but skilled professionals are crucial to transforming that data into actionable insights. By filtering out the noise and highlighting key information, data specialists enable smarter, data-driven decisions, making AI a valuable asset in your strategic planning.

(iv) **Prioritizing Privacy and Security:**
Data privacy and security are paramount when working with AI. Big data and AI experts know how to safeguard sensitive information during processing and storage, protecting your business from data breaches and ensuring regulatory compliance.

While big data holds immense potential, its true value only emerges when handled by knowledgeable professionals. Without data expertise, the complexity of big data can feel overwhelming. But with the right experts, AI's complexity becomes clarity, empowering you to make smarter decisions that enhance operational efficiency and give you a competitive edge in the market. Embrace AI—guided by skilled hands—and unlock the full potential of your business!

"You can have data without information, but you cannot have information without data."
— *Daniel Keys Moran, Computer Programmer and Entrepreneur*

Chapter 3
AI's Evolution – From Vision to Everyday Impact

The journey of artificial intelligence is one of visionary ideas, technological advancements, and transformative breakthroughs. From its early days in the 1950s to the cutting-edge generative AI we see today, AI has evolved through three significant "booms" that have reshaped industries, redefined human-computer interaction, and sparked philosophical and ethical debates. This essay explores the fascinating progression of AI, highlighting each phase of growth and the technological milestones that brought AI from theory to an integral part of our daily lives.

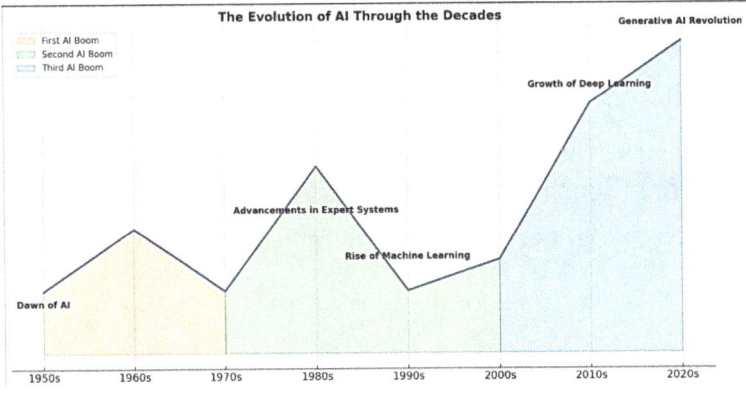

Figure 2: A decade-by-decade overview of AI's evolution from the 1950s to the 2020s. (Illustration by Dr. Koay)

The Emergence of 1950s AI

British mathematician Alan Turing revolutionized discussions on artificial intelligence with his groundbreaking paper Computing Machinery and Intelligence, published in Mind. In this pivotal work, Turing tackled the question, "Can machines think?" by proposing an innovative approach to reframe the debate. Instead of directly defining "thinking," he introduced the concept of the "imitation game," later known as the Turing Test.

The Turing Test evaluates whether a machine can exhibit behaviour so convincingly human-like that it becomes indistinguishable from a person during interaction. By shifting the focus to observable outcomes rather than abstract definitions, Turing provided a practical framework for studying machine intelligence. His ideas not only laid the groundwork for modern AI research but also inspired ongoing discussions about the nature of intelligence and the limits of machine capability. The Turing Test remains an enduring benchmark for assessing AI's ability to replicate human thought and communication[2].

---

[2] https://www.ibm.com/think/topics/history-of-artificial-intelligence

Figure 3: Alan Turing's accomplishments included helping invent a device that could crack secret codes sent by German armed forces that were sent via "Enigma" machines. (Source: Qualcomm[3])

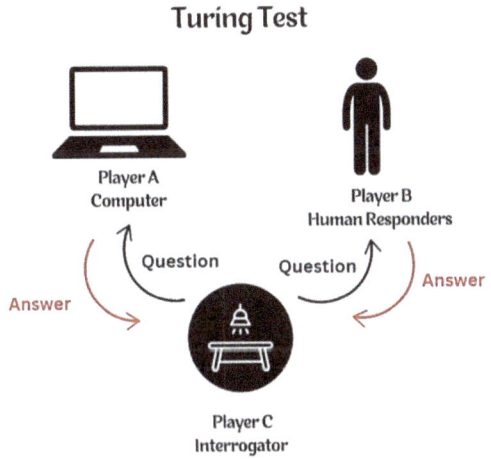

Figure 4: Turing Test. During the Turing Test, the human interrogator asks several questions to both players. Based on the answers, the interrogator attempts to determine which players are a computer and which players is a human respondent. (Illustration by Dr. Koay)

---

[3]https://www.qualcomm.com/news/onq/2024/02/the-rise-of-generative-ai-timeline-of-breakthrough- innovations

Figure 5 : Alan Turing (1912-1954)[4]. (Photo Source: History Extra)

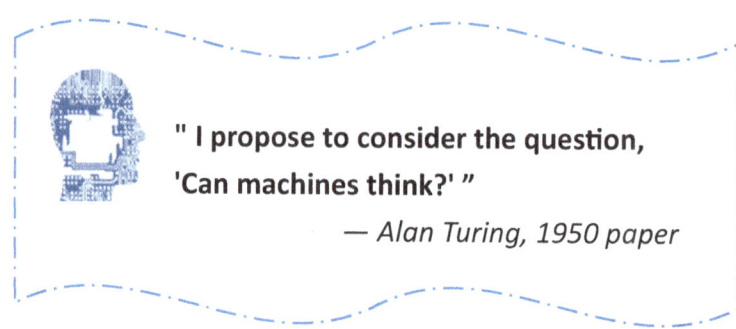

" I propose to consider the question, 'Can machines think?' "

— *Alan Turing, 1950 paper*

In 1956, the concept of "artificial intelligence" was officially born at the Dartmouth Conference, where a group of visionary scientists gathered to explore the idea of giving machines human-like intelligence. It was as if a scene from

---

[4] https://www.historyextra.com/period/second-world-war/alan-turing-life-death-legacy-facts-enigma- sexuality-timeline/

a sci-fi movie had come to life—these pioneers were brainstorming ways to create machines that could truly "think" and act intelligently. This meeting marked a turning point, setting ambitious goals that would inspire decades of innovation in the quest to bring human-like capabilities to technology[5].

Figure 6: In the 1956 Dartmouth AI workshop photo: (back row, from left) Oliver Selfridge, Nathaniel Rochester, Marvin Minsky, and John McCarthy; (front row, from left) Ray Solomonoff, Pete Milner, and Claude Shannon. Photo courtesy of the Minsky family[6] (Source: The University of Sydney).

---

[5] https://home.dartmouth.edu/about/artificial-intelligence-ai-coined-dartmouth#:~:text=1956,artificial%20intelligence%20as%20a%20field.&text=In%201956%2C%20a%20small%20group,of%20this%20field%20of%20research.
[6] https://www.sydney.edu.au/news-opinion/news/2024/09/02/ai-was-born-at-a-us-summer-camp-68-years-ago.html

A PROPOSAL FOR THE DARTMOUTH SUMMER RESEARCH PROJECT ON ARTIFICIAL INTELLIGENCE

J. McCarthy, Dartmouth College
M. L. Minsky, Harvard University
N. Rochester, I.B.M. Corporation
C.E. Shannon, Bell Telephone Laboratories

August 31, 1955

We propose that a 2 month, 10 man study of artificial intelligence be carried out during the summer of 1956 at Dartmouth College in Hanover, New Hampshire. The study is to proceed on the basis of the conjecture that every aspect of learning or any other feature of intelligence can in principle be so precisely described that a machine can be made to simulate it. An attempt will be made to find how to make machines use language, form abstractions and concepts, solve kinds of problems now reserved for humans, and improve themselves. We think that a significant advance can be made in one or more of these problems if a carefully selected group of scientists work on it together for a summer.

The following are some aspects of the artificial intelligence problem: 1

Automatic Computers

If a machine can do a job, then an automatic calculator can be programmed to simulate the machine. The speeds and memory capacities of present computers may be insufficient to simulate many of the higher functions of the human brain, but the major obstacle is not lack of machine capacity, but our inability to write programs taking full advantage of what we have. 2.

How Can a Computer be Programmed to Use a Language

It may be speculated that a large part of human thought consists of manipulating words according to rules of reasoning and rules of conjecture. From this point of view, forming a generalization consists of admitting a new word and some rules whereby sentences containing it imply and are implied by others. This idea has never been very precisely formulated nor have examples been worked out.

3. **Neuron Nets**

How can a set of (hypothetical) neurons be arranged so as to form concepts. Considerable theoretical and experimental work has been done on this problem by Uttley, Rashevsky and his group, Farley and Clark, Pitts and McCulloch,

Figure 7: A Proposal for the Dartmouth Summer Research Project on Artificial Intelligence (1955)[7].

Early AI systems, like ELIZA from the 1960s, could engage in conversations but felt like chatting with a not-so-smart robot. A few simple exchanges worked, but getting it

---

[7]https://www.formal.stanford.edu/jmc/history/dartmouth.pdf?ref=cantorsparadise.org

to grasp complex contexts was a whole different ball game. Back then, AI was like a student who could only recite memorized lines but lacked genuine understanding.

```
Talk to Eliza by typing your questions and answers in the input box.
> Hello, I am Eliza. I'll be your therapist today.
* Hi, may I know what is your name?
> Have you asked anyone else?
* May I know what therapist that you can do for me?
> We were discussing you, not me.
* Sorry?
> Apologies are not necessary.




TYPE HERE
```

Figure 8: A demonstration of how Eliza responds to open-ended questions[8]

AI: Exploration and Limits (1960s-1980s)

As the years passed, scientists began building increasingly sophisticated "expert systems" to tackle specialized tasks. A standout example is MYCIN, an early AI program developed at Stanford University in 1972 to help doctors diagnose blood infections. MYCIN analysed patient-reported symptoms and medical test results to provide preliminary diagnostic guidance[9]. Once given a patient's symptoms and test outcomes, the system would process the data and suggest a diagnosis. However, these early systems

---

[8] https://web.njit.edu/~ronkowit/eliza.html
[9] https://www.britannica.com/technology/MYCIN

operated like a chef bound to a strict recipe—they excelled at specific tasks but were confined to a rigid set of rules. When confronted with anything beyond their programmed framework, they would simply stall, much like a chef lost without a recipe to follow.

By the late 1970s, AI hit a development bottleneck. Funding for research dwindled, and AI didn't seem as magical to the public anymore. This period is often referred to as the "AI winter," as the technology faced limitations and failed to dazzle as expected, causing enthusiasm to wane.

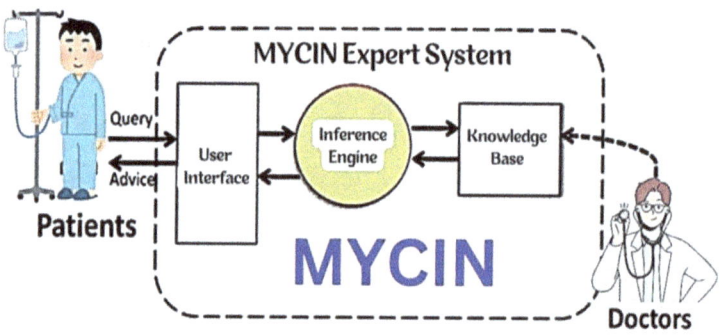

Figure 9: MYCIN Expert System. (Illustration by Dr. Koay)

Neural Networks Reborn: 1980s-2000s

The next major leap in AI was driven by the revival of neural networks, transforming how machines learn. Imagine AI as a young learner, growing smarter with practice. In 1986, David Rumelhart, Geoffrey Hinton, and Ronald Williams introduced backpropagation—a revolutionary algorithm that reshaped the field [10]. This method allowed neural networks to adjust weights in multiple layers, making it possible for them to tackle complex, non-linear challenges.

Back-propagation was a turning point, giving AI a practical way to train deep neural networks. This wasn't just rote memorization anymore; AI could adapt and refine its skills over time. With Back-propagation, AI learned to recognize speech, decipher handwritten text, interpret images, and even understand spoken conversations— paving the way for many of today's machine learning applications.

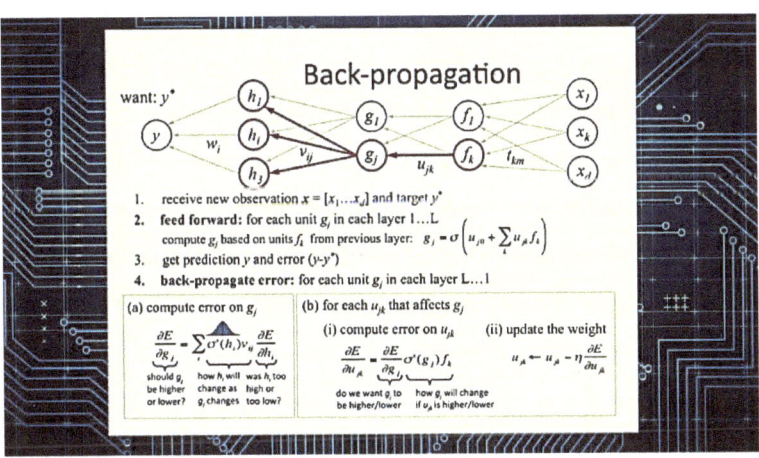

---

[10] https://www.nature.com/articles/323533a0

Figure 10: The Back-propagation[11].

During this time, AI started dipping its toes into areas like voice and handwriting recognition. While its performance was far from what we have today, it laid the groundwork for our future smart assistants. Imagine chatting with Siri today; while it understands your commands, if you went back to the '80s, it might only comprehend simple commands like "turn on the light" or "turn off the light."

Deep Learning Boom: 2000s-2020s

Machine learning lies at the heart of these capabilities, enhancing the intelligence of Siri, Alexa, and Google Assistant to feel almost human. Machine learning is an AI application that focuses on teaching systems to improve continuously by learning from data, enabling them to perform better over time. With this method, these AI-powered assistants can analyse data patterns, learning to make future decisions without needing step-by-step programming. And with advancements in natural language processing and deep learning, conversational AI is closer to replicating human interaction than ever.

---

[11] https://randomresearchai.medium.com/backpropagation-high-school-student-edition-11c8f77419c9

Every time Siri, Alexa, or Google Assistant makes an error or nails a response, it's a learning moment. By analysing whether their answers were accurate or missed the mark, they adjust and refine their approach, improving with each interaction. In this way, virtual assistants develop a "rulebook" of what works, constantly guiding them toward greater accuracy in future conversations.

The modern era of deep learning took a historic turn on September 30, 2012. On this day, a Convolutional Neural Network (CNN) named AlexNet entered the ImageNet challenge and redefined the field. AlexNet didn't just win—it dominated. Standing out from its competitors, AlexNet conquered the largest image dataset of its time, beating the closest model by a margin of 9.8 percentage point. This accomplishment didn't just secure AlexNet's place as a breakthrough; it marked a turning point, propelling AI into mainstream attention[12].

What made AlexNet so remarkable was its design. With eight layers—five convolutional and three fully connected—it introduced a new standard for neural networks. By implementing ReLU activations, AlexNet achieved a 25% error rate on the CIFAR-10 dataset, performing six times faster than previous models that used the tanh activation function. Credit goes to Krizhevsky and

---

[12] https://www.pinecone.io/learn/series/image-search/imagenet/

colleagues, the creators behind AlexNet's pioneering design[12].

Beyond its impact on computer vision, AlexNet inspired applications in fields like natural language processing and medical imaging, establishing deep learning as a transformative tool across industries. As AI continues to advance, AlexNet's revolutionary architecture may inspire the next generation of models, signalling a future where AI's potential knows no bounds.

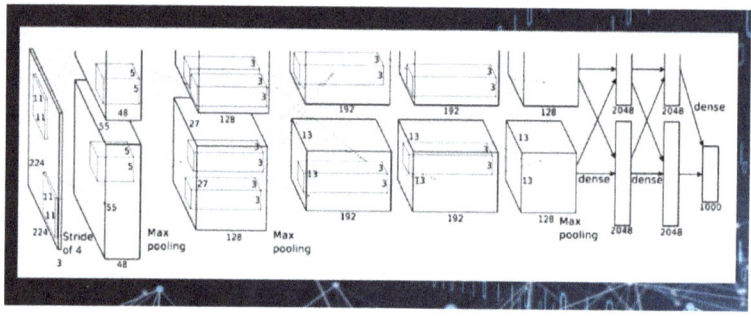

Figure 11: Convolutional Neural Networks that use ReLU achieved a 25% error rate on CIFAR-10 six times faster than those that used tanh. Image credits to Krizhevsky et al., the original authors of the AlexNet paper[13].

---

[13] https://towardsdatascience.com/alexnet-the-architecture-that-challenged-cnns-e406d5297951

Generative AI: 2020s & Beyond

The emergence of generative artificial intelligence (AI) has ushered in a transformative era, reshaping industries and redefining human-computer interaction. From its early AI foundations to its rapid growth in the 2020s, generative AI has become a hub of innovation, creativity, and ethical debate.

The Foundations of Generative AI

Generative AI refers to algorithms capable of creating new content—whether text, images, audio, or video—by learning from existing data patterns. This journey began with breakthroughs in machine learning and neural networks. Early models like Variational Autoencoders (VAEs) and Generative Adversarial Networks (GANs) laid the groundwork, enabling machines to learn from data distributions and produce realistic outputs[14].

The introduction of transformer architectures in 2017 transformed natural language processing (NLP). Models such as GPT-1 and its successors, including GPT-3 and GPT-4, demonstrated unparalleled abilities in generating coherent and contextually relevant text. These advances

---

[14] https://en.wikipedia.org/wiki/Generative_artificial_intelligence

paved the way for generative AI's widespread application across various industries[15].

Key Milestones (The 2020 and beyond)

The progression of generative AI from 2020 to 2024 is marked by several groundbreaking moments:

2020: OpenAI launched GPT-3, boasting 175 billion parameters that set new standards for text generation. This year also saw a surge in applications using AI for everything from content creation to coding assistance[16].

2021: The debut of DALL-E by OpenAI showcased the potential to generate images from textual descriptions, marking a major leap in multimodal AI applications. With simple prompts, users could now create visual content, signalling a new era for creative AI[15].

2022: ChatGPT brought generative AI into mainstream awareness with a user-friendly interface that empowered businesses and individuals to use AI for customer service, content creation, and more. This year also raised concerns over misinformation and ethical issues surrounding AI-generated content[16].

---

[15] https://www.techtarget.com/searchenterpriseai/tip/The-history-of-artificial-intelligence-Complete-AI-timeline
[16] https://www.ibm.com/topics/generative-ai

2023: The release of GPT-4 further expanded generative AI capabilities, allowing for multimodal inputs (text and images) and a stronger contextual understanding. Companies began integrating these models into their operations, driving efficiency and fostering innovation[17].

2024: A McKinsey survey revealed that 65% of companies were now regularly utilizing generative AI tools. This year highlighted the critical need for ethical frameworks as businesses navigated generative AI's rapid expansion and its complex challenges[17].

The rise of generative AI from 2020 to 2024 reflects a remarkable technological evolution with profound societal implications. As organizations explore its vast potential, balancing innovation with ethical considerations remains crucial. The future holds promise for even greater advancements that could redefine creativity, productivity, and how we interact with technology.

"We are moving from a world where we have to understand how to use machines to a world where the machines understand us."
— Ginni Rometty, Former CEO of IBM

---

[17] https://www.mckinsey.com/capabilities/quantumblack/our-insights/the-state-of-ai

Chapter 4

From Traditional AI to Generative AI

Artificial Intelligence has rapidly advanced, evolving from traditional systems designed for specific tasks to generative AI capable of creating and innovating. This progression highlights a shift from automation-focused solutions to dynamic, adaptable technologies that reshape how we solve problems and approach creativity in various industries.

Traditional AI: Rule-Based Simplicity

Traditional AI can be compared to a "highly intelligent but narrowly focused assistant." It is adept at handling specific tasks, but only when guided by a well-defined set of rules and procedures. This type of AI resembles older mobile phones—capable in its own right, yet confined to a limited range of functions. For instance, while an old flip phone can manage calls and texts effectively, it lacks the ability to download applications, browse social media, navigate maps, or take high-definition photos like modern smartphones[18]. Similarly, traditional AI excels at specific tasks but falters when confronted with scenarios outside its established parameters.

---

[18] Russell, S., & Norvig, P. (2020). Artificial Intelligence: A Modern Approach. Pearson.

Rule-Based Systems: The Logic Expert of "If... Then..."

At the core of traditional AI lies a logic framework based on "if... then..." rules, which function as pre-defined conditional responses[19]. For example, you can establish a series of rules for the AI to follow, allowing it to execute tasks automatically based on those guidelines. Picture yourself working at a bank and monitoring unusual transaction activities. Traditional AI would act like a diligent detective, adhering to your rules: "If an account shows frequent withdrawals within a short time frame, then trigger an alert." This efficiency stems from the AI's ability to follow established protocols; however, when faced with situations that fall outside these predefined conditions, it becomes ineffective and unable to respond appropriately.

---

[19] Luger, G. F., & Stubblefield, W. A. (2009). Artificial Intelligence: Structures and Strategies for Complex Problem Solving. Pearson.

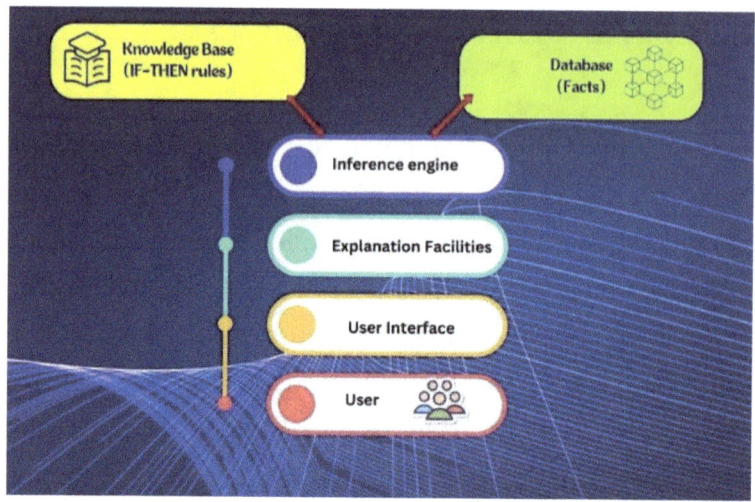

Figure 12: Rule Base Expert System (Illustration by Dr. Koay)

Example: House Cleaning Robot

Consider a cleaning robot programmed with simple instructions: "If there is trash on the floor, activate the vacuum." Whenever it detects debris, it starts cleaning automatically. This illustrates how traditional AI operates—it performs tasks effectively under predetermined conditions. However, if you accidentally spill water and the robot isn't programmed to recognize spills, it may remain idle, waiting for "trash" to appear because it lacks the capability to understand or react to this new situation[20].

---

[20] Boden, M. A. (2016). AI: Its Nature and Future. Oxford University Press.

Experts in Specialized Fields: Masters of Specific Skills

Another defining feature of traditional AI is its proficiency in specialized areas. It can excel in one domain but struggles significantly when asked to operate outside that realm. This is akin to a chef who can masterfully prepare pasta but is completely out of their depth when tasked with making sushi. While AI can become highly skilled in a particular field, its performance may decline sharply if required to handle different types of tasks[21].

Example: Medical Diagnosis AI

In the medical sector, for instance, some AI systems are trained on thousands of X-ray images to identify lung diseases accurately. This system performs exceptionally well at detecting lung abnormalities. However, if you were to ask this AI to analyze other types of medical images, such as brain CT scans, it would likely struggle and fail to provide accurate diagnoses due to its lack of training in that area[22].

---

[21] Goodfellow, I., Bengio, Y., & Courville, A. (2016). Deep Learning. MIT Press.
[22] Esteva, A., Kuprel, B., Novoa, R. A., Wang, S., et al. (2019). "Dermatologist-level classification of skin cancer with deep neural networks." Nature, 542(7639), 115-118.

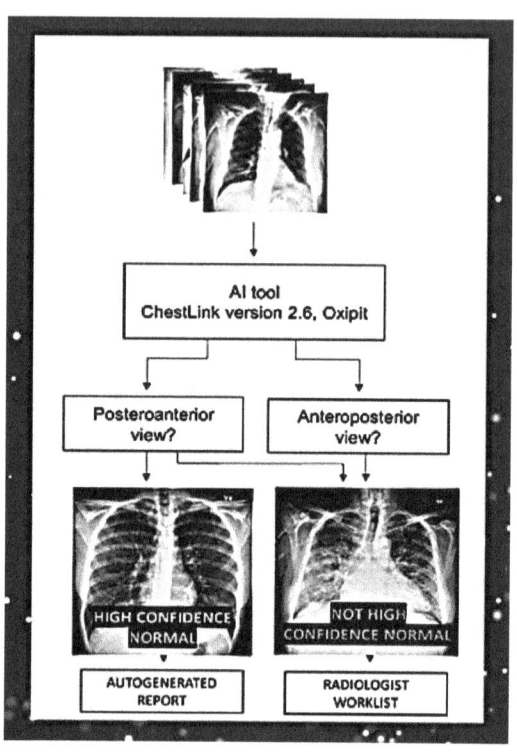

Figure 13: Flowchart for Chest X-ray Classification Using an AI Tool[23]. (Image source: RSNA[23])

Posteroanterior and lateral chest X-ray images are analysed by the AI tool, while prior chest X-rays are excluded from this process. The AI classifies each image as either "high confidence normal" or "not high confidence normal," indicating "normal" and "abnormal" as referenced in the main text. In cases where the AI determines a "normal" result, an automated report may be generated, labelled as "normal chest radiograph[23]."

---

[23] https://healthcare-in-europe.com/en/news/ai-identifies-normal-abnormal-chest-x-rays.html

Decision Trees: The Step-by-Step Thinker

Traditional AI also excels in utilizing "decision trees," which function like a logical thinker who systematically narrows down options step by step to arrive at the most suitable answer[24]. Each question or scenario follows a set sequence for resolution; rather than jumping to conclusions, it analyses one step at a time.

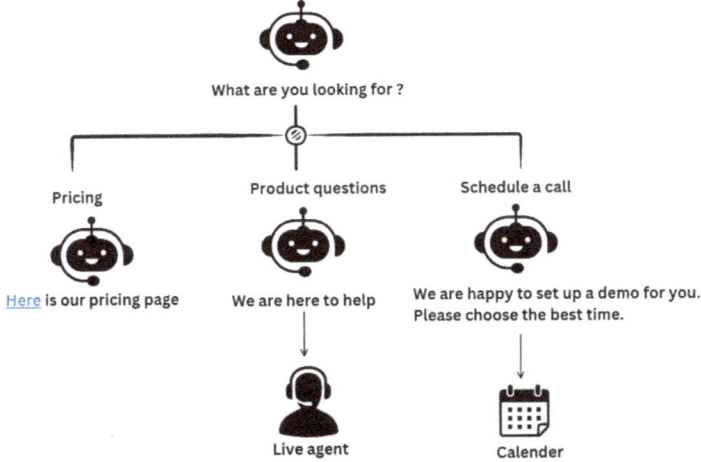

Figure 14: Example of Chatbot Decision Tree for Customer Assistance. This diagram illustrates a chatbot decision tree, guiding users through structured paths for customer support options. (Illustration by Dr. Koay)

---

[24] Quinlan, J. R. (1986). "Induction of Decision Trees." Machine Learning, 1(1), 81-106.

Example: Ordering at a Restaurant

Imagine entering a restaurant where the waiter asks you questions like, "Do you prefer beef or chicken? Would you like salad or mashed potatoes?" These seemingly simple inquiries form a "decision tree." Your choices guide you toward a customized meal. Traditional AI operates similarly; it narrows down options through a series of rules and decisions to provide an answer. In the insurance sector, for example, AI employs this decision tree method to evaluate customer risk by sifting through data such as age, income, and health status[25]. While this approach works well for routine scenarios, traditional AI often struggles with unexpected situations and finds it challenging to adapt.

Statistical Modelling and Optimization

Traditional artificial intelligence (AI) can manage extensive datasets, performing statistical analyses, and optimizing decision-making processes. For example, banks utilize AI to compute customer credit scores by swiftly analysing income and spending patterns, thus generating scores that inform loan approval decisions[26].

---

[25] Breiman, L., Friedman, J. H., Olshen, R. A., & Stone, C. J. (1986). Classification and Regression Trees. Wadsworth.
[26] https://www.bacancytechnology.com/blog/ai-credit-scoring

Example: AI Revolutionizes Credit Scoring

Imagine a credit scoring system that doesn't just rely on traditional metrics but taps into a vast network of data to paint a fuller picture of financial trustworthiness. That's the power of AI in credit scoring. By analysing diverse datasets from various sources, AI transforms raw financial information into meaningful insights. For banks and lenders, this means smarter, faster, and more dynamic credit assessments. Here's a look at how AI harnesses data to make precise predictions and drive informed, actionable decisions in the world of finance[26].

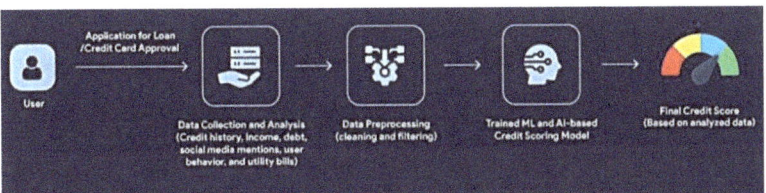

Figure 15: How AI-Driven Credit Scoring Works? (Source: BACANCY[26])

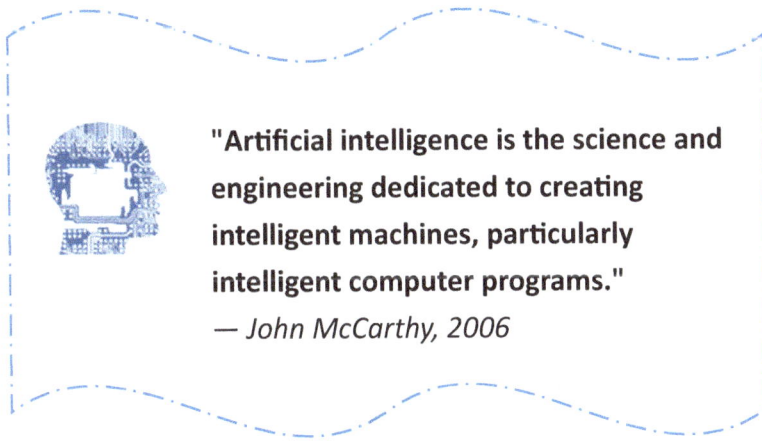

"Artificial intelligence is the science and engineering dedicated to creating intelligent machines, particularly intelligent computer programs."
— *John McCarthy, 2006*

Generative AI: Rise & Impact

Generative AI marks a transformative leap in the field of artificial intelligence, enabling machines to create entirely new content—ranging from text and images to audio and synthetic data—by analyzing and learning from extensive datasets. This capability sets generative AI apart from traditional AI, which primarily focuses on classifying, interpreting, or processing existing information [27]. By leveraging large foundational models, such as large language models (LLMs), generative AI excels at producing original content that reflects the patterns and nuances found within its training data[28].

What are Large Language Models (LLMs)?

LLMs are sophisticated AI systems designed to process and generate text. They leverage deep learning techniques, particularly the transformer architecture, which allows them to analyze context and relationships between words effectively. This architecture was introduced in the influential paper "Attention Is All You Need" by Vaswani et al. in 2017[29], marking a significant advancement in NLP technology.

---

[27] Baker et al., "The Role of Artificial Intelligence in Modern Society," Nature, 2023.
[28] Radford et al., "Language Models are Unsupervised Multitask Learners," OpenAI, 2019
[29] https://proceedings.neurips.cc/paper_files/paper/2017/file/3f5ee243547dee91fbd053c1c4a845aa-Paper.pdf

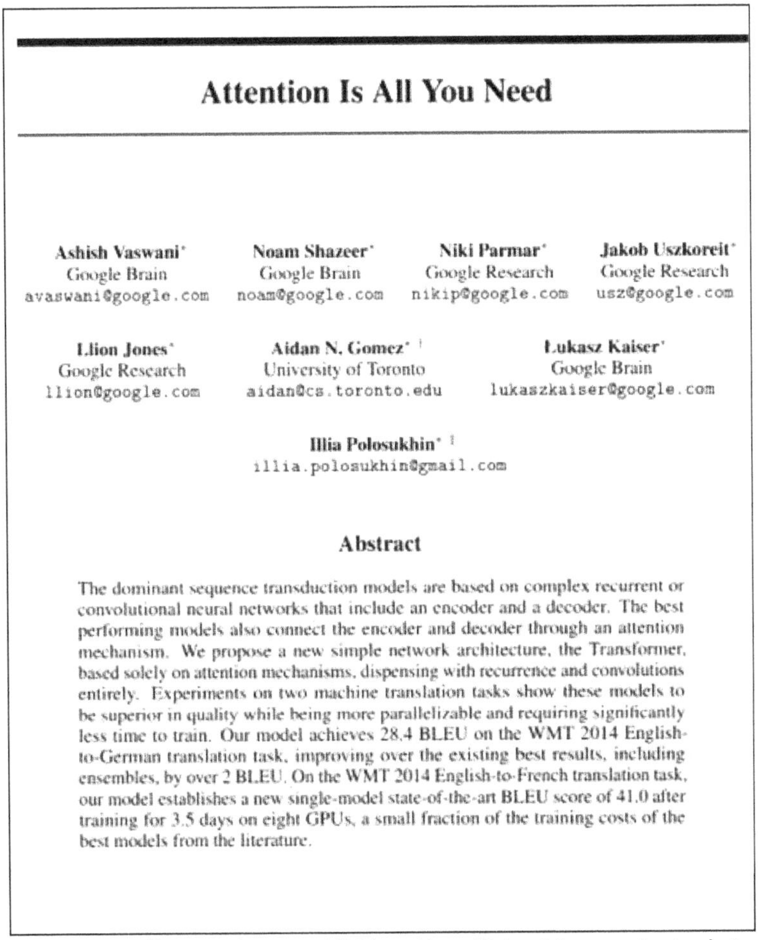

> # Attention Is All You Need
>
> **Ashish Vaswani**[*]
> Google Brain
> avaswani@google.com
>
> **Noam Shazeer**[*]
> Google Brain
> noam@google.com
>
> **Niki Parmar**[*]
> Google Research
> nikip@google.com
>
> **Jakob Uszkoreit**[*]
> Google Research
> usz@google.com
>
> **Llion Jones**[*]
> Google Research
> llion@google.com
>
> **Aidan N. Gomez**[*][†]
> University of Toronto
> aidan@cs.toronto.edu
>
> **Lukasz Kaiser**[*]
> Google Brain
> lukaszkaiser@google.com
>
> **Illia Polosukhin**[*][‡]
> illia.polosukhin@gmail.com
>
> ## Abstract
>
> The dominant sequence transduction models are based on complex recurrent or convolutional neural networks that include an encoder and a decoder. The best performing models also connect the encoder and decoder through an attention mechanism. We propose a new simple network architecture, the Transformer, based solely on attention mechanisms, dispensing with recurrence and convolutions entirely. Experiments on two machine translation tasks show these models to be superior in quality while being more parallelizable and requiring significantly less time to train. Our model achieves 28.4 BLEU on the WMT 2014 English-to-German translation task, improving over the existing best results, including ensembles, by over 2 BLEU. On the WMT 2014 English-to-French translation task, our model establishes a new single-model state-of-the-art BLEU score of 41.0 after training for 3.5 days on eight GPUs, a small fraction of the training costs of the best models from the literature.

Figure 16: "Attention Is All You Need" by Vaswani et al. in 2017[29].

Key Features of LLMs

(i) Scale: LLMs typically contain billions of parameters. For instance, OpenAI's GPT-3 model has 175 billion parameters, enabling it to learn complex language patterns from extensive datasets.

(ii) Contextual Understanding: Unlike earlier models that processed text sequentially, transformers can evaluate entire sentences or paragraphs at once. This ability allows them to grasp nuanced meanings and relationships between distant words.

(iii) Generative Capabilities: LLMs can produce coherent and contextually relevant text based on prompts. This makes them suitable for various tasks, including writing essays, generating code, and creating conversational agents.

How LLMs Are Trained?

Large Language Models (LLMs) "learn" in a structured, progressive way, with each stage of training sharpening their capabilities. The journey begins with pre-training, where the model is exposed to vast amounts of data—both unlabelled public data and unique proprietary data. In this phase, LLMs learn foundational language patterns and associations without human guidance, absorbing an extensive understanding of language.

Next comes fine-tuning, a more focused phase where the model receives narrower, high-quality datasets and benefits from human feedback. This step refines the model's responses, making them more accurate, context-aware, and aligned with specific goals or ethical standards.

In some cases, a third stage, specialized prompting, further enhances the model. Here, experts use targeted prompts and instructions to guide the model toward performing specialized tasks, like coding assistance or scientific analysis. This tailored approach transforms the LLM from a general language model into a powerful tool for specific applications, finely tuned to meet unique requirements.

Through these stages, LLMs evolve from general learners into versatile and highly capable models ready to tackle complex, domain-specific challenges.

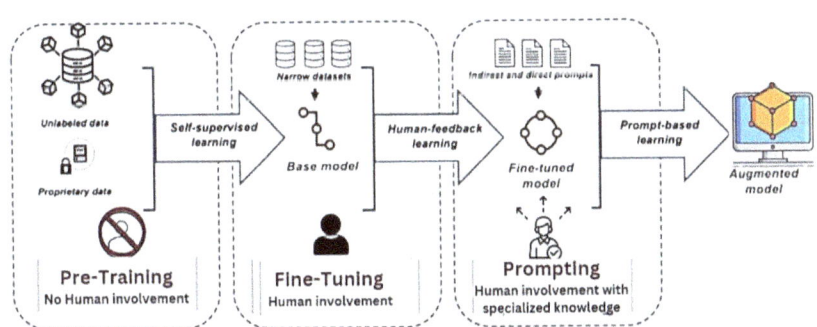

Figure 17: Overview of the LLM Training Process (Illustration by Dr. Koay)

Example of Training

For instance, when provided with the phrase "The cat," LLM would predict the next word in the sequence, generating "sat.". If a model is trained with the sentence "The cat sat on the...", it learns to predict that "mat" is a likely next word based on context derived from its training data.

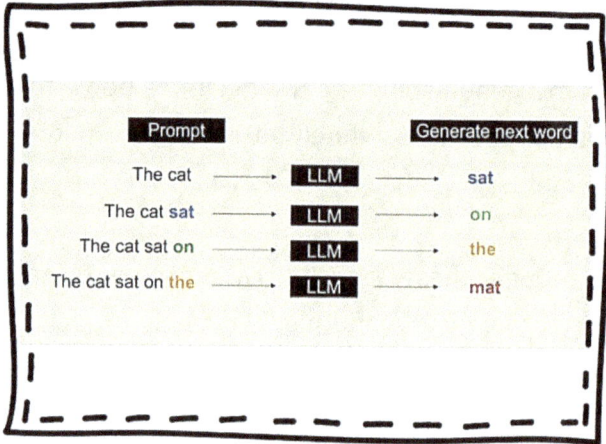

Figure 18: Example of Training (Illustration by Dr. Koay)

Milestones in Generative AI Development

The evolution of generative AI has been marked by several key milestones that illustrate its rapid advancement:
- ChatGPT by OpenAI (2022): Launched in November 2022, ChatGPT quickly gained popularity for its ability to engage in coherent conversations and generate contextually relevant text across various styles and formats. Initially powered by OpenAI's

GPT-3.5 model, it set a new standard for conversational agents[30].
- LLaMA by Meta (2023): Meta's LLaMA introduced powerful open-source language models that deliver advanced capabilities while requiring lower computational resources. Its potential was demonstrated through on-device implementations compatible with mobile hardware[31].
- PaLM and Gemini by Google: Google's Pathways Language Model (PaLM) and its successor Gemini represent significant breakthroughs in natural language processing. Gemini offers multi-modal capabilities across text, code, audio, and images while emphasizing safety and ethical considerations in its applications[32].
- BLOOM (2022): Developed by BigScience, BLOOM is an open-source multilingual model that supports 46 languages and 13 programming languages. With 176 billion parameters, it democratizes access to advanced language processing technologies for smaller enterprises and researchers[33].
- Text-to-Image Models: Innovations like OpenAI's DALL-E have revolutionized visual content creation. DALL-E, a proprietary tool, generates images directly

---

[30] https://openai.com/index/chatgpt/
[31] https://ai.meta.com/blog/
[32] https://research.google/blog/
[33] https://bigscience.huggingface.co/blog/bloom

from textual prompts, opening new possibilities for creative expression[34].

Generative AI vs. Traditional AI?

To fully appreciate the significance of generative AI, it is essential to understand how it operates in contrast to traditional AI systems:

Learning Mechanism
• Traditional AI: Traditional AI systems rely heavily on predefined algorithms and rule-based approaches. These systems are typically designed for specific tasks, such as classification or regression, and require human intervention to update their rules based on new data. This can lead to limitations in adaptability and responsiveness[35].
• Generative AI: In contrast, generative AI employs advanced deep learning techniques, particularly neural networks, to analyse vast datasets. These models learn from the data by identifying complex patterns and relationships, allowing them to generate new content autonomously. This self-learning capability enables generative AI to adapt and improve continuously without the need for constant human oversight[36].

---

[34] https://openai.com/index/dall-e/
[35] Russell & Norvig, Artificial Intelligence: A Modern Approach, Pearson Education Limited, 2020
[36] Vaswani et al., "Attention is All You Need," arXiv, 2017

Output Capabilities

• Traditional AI: The primary function of traditional AI is to process existing data. It excels at tasks such as sorting information, making predictions based on historical data, and providing insights through data analysis. However, it lacks the ability to create new content or ideas[37].

• Generative AI: Generative AI is capable of producing novel outputs across various mediums—text, images, music, and even code. For instance, it can generate a unique piece of art based on a textual description or compose music that adheres to specified themes. This creative output showcases a level of originality that traditional systems cannot achieve[38].

Flexibility and Adaptability

• Traditional AI: Often characterized by rigidity, traditional AI systems struggle to adapt to unforeseen scenarios or changes in context without manual reprogramming. Their performance is typically limited to the specific tasks for which they were designed[39].

• Generative AI: Generative models are inherently more flexible and capable of handling complex and dynamic situations. By learning from diverse datasets, they can generate contextually relevant responses or creative

---

[37] Goodfellow et al., Deep Learning, MIT Press, 2016.
[38] Elgammal et al., "Can Machines Be Creative?," Proceedings of the IEEE, 2017
[39] Manning et al., Introduction to Information Retrieval, Stanford University Press, 2008

outputs even in novel scenarios. This adaptability makes generative AI particularly valuable in rapidly changing environments[40].

 *" Humans know what other humans want. Humans are going to have better tools. We've had better tools before, but we're still very focused on each other. "*
— *Sam Altman, CEO, OpenAI*

---

[40] Bengio et al., "Learning Deep Architectures for AI," Foundations and Trends® in Machine Learning, 2013.

Chapter 5

Generative AI: Shaping Smart Cities

While artificial intelligence has already transformed urban centres into smart cities, some have started to integrate generative AI (gen AI) to amplify their operations. As cities evolve, so does their technology, and gen AI is becoming a game-changer in enhancing urban life and governance.

The G20 Global Smart Cities Alliance, in partnership with the World Economic Forum, laid out guiding principles for the responsible adoption of smart city tech. With gen AI, cities can now move beyond data analytics and automation to introduce capabilities that were previously unimaginable. But just how ready are cities worldwide to adopt this transformative technology?

In a survey conducted by Bloomberg Philanthropies in 2023, 96% of surveyed mayors around the world expressed interest in using Gen AI[41], but only 2% of mayors reported actively using gen AI, even though nine out of ten expressed interests according to a Bloomberg Philanthropies survey from 2023[41]. For most cities, this is still an emerging

---

[41] https://cityaiconnect.jhu.edu/pdfs/Final-Gen-AI-In-Cities-Report_10.18.2023.pdf

technology, and there's a learning curve in implementing it effectively. Yet, a handful of cities are taking bold steps, exploring ways to bring AI-driven innovations into their communities.

Here's a look at how five pioneering cities is embracing gen AI and transforming their urban landscapes:

Buenos Aires: Chatbots for Public Service

In Buenos Aires, Argentina, the city's official chatbot, "Boti," has evolved with generative AI since its launch in 2019[42]. Originally deployed to streamline public services and support COVID-19 testing, Boti now supports a wide range of services from social care to bike-sharing. In January 2022 alone, it recorded over 11 million conversations, making it a preferred contact point for citizens[42]. With Boti, 82% of queries are solved by chatbots, with only 18% being referred to human agents[43]. Boti's success demonstrates how generative AI can empower city governments to stay connected with residents in real-time.

---

[42] https://www.weforum.org/stories/2024/07/generative-ai-smart-cities/
[43] https://botmaker.com/en/clients/boti-caba-bot

Singapore: Innovating Services & Workforce

Singapore has emerged as a global leader in integrating generative AI into public and private sectors, leveraging over 100 generative AI solutions as part of its revised National AI Strategy. At the forefront is Singapore's pioneering digital twin—a virtual model of the city-state— and a government-led initiative focused on rapid AI adoption across diverse applications. This initiative has already driven advancements such as a generative AI-powered content tool for educators and a chatbot for community centres, providing practical AI-driven solutions to improve service delivery[44].

In line with the National AI Strategy, Singapore has adopted a progressive approach, encouraging not only the responsible integration of AI but also economic embrace. The city-state's commitment to harnessing AI for economic growth has led to an interdisciplinary research group of MIT professors exploring human-machine synergy to enhance Singapore's AI ecosystem.

An essential part of this initiative, the "AI Trailblazers" program, launched in collaboration with the Ministry of Communications and Information (MCI), Digital Industry

---

[44] https://www.straitstimes.com/tech/tech-news/more-than-100-solutions-developed-as-part-of-generative-ai-initiative?close=true

Singapore (DISG), Smart Nation and Digital Government Office (SNDGO), and Google Cloud, aims to drive generative AI innovation through targeted support. The AI Trailblazers program, introduced on July 24, 2023, is designed to address real-world challenges by creating dedicated "Innovation Sandboxes" for the public and private sectors. These Sandboxes offer over 100 organizations-controlled access to Google Cloud's generative AI resources, including advanced graphical processing units (GPUs), the Vertex AI platform, and low-code tools, enabling seamless AI experimentation within a secure cloud environment[45].

To build in-house expertise, participants in the AI Trailblazers program undergo intensive workshops and hands-on training with Google Cloud engineers. These sessions guide participants in developing prototype solutions that can be further refined into minimum viable products (MVPs) and showcased at an AI Trailblazers Awards ceremony, ensuring that promising solutions are recognized and prepared for scalable deployment[45].

Further solidifying the public-private partnership, the AI Trailblazers initiative falls under MCI and Google Cloud's broader collaboration, which spans four pillars. In addition to the AI Trailblazers, future pillars will include programs focused on AI skill development, the growth of home-grown

---

[45] https://www.smartnation.gov.sg/media-hub/press-releases/24072023/

AI startups, and initiatives promoting Responsible AI. This partnership seeks to embed ethical standards, as seen through Google Cloud's involvement in IMDA's AI Verify Foundation, which promotes responsible AI practices and aims to establish Singapore as a trusted AI hub[45].

The AI Trailblazers program and the broader collaboration between MCI and Google Cloud underscore Singapore's ambition to position itself as an AI-driven economy that embraces innovation and ethical standards. Through initiatives like these, Singapore aims to empower organizations to develop impactful, secure, and accessible generative AI solutions, setting an example for nations worldwide in responsibly accelerating digital transformation[45].

Amsterdam: AI for Sustainable Materials

In Amsterdam, the innovative use of generative AI has taken a revolutionary turn, moving from the digital to the molecular realm. Researchers at the University of Amsterdam (UvA) have initiated the Artificial Intelligence for Sustainable Molecules and Materials (AI4SMM) project, focusing on developing eco-friendly molecules that could pave the way for a greener, more sustainable future. By applying techniques originally devised for language models like ChatGPT, scientists are now "teaching" AI to comprehend molecular interactions and create entirely new materials[46].

Bernd Ensing, a leading professor at UvA's Faculty of Science, explains the vision behind AI4SMM: to empower chemists with AI tools that facilitate material creation, removing some reliance on "chemical intuition." As Ensing notes, AI's generative modelling can enable researchers to explore new substances without manual experimentation, bringing a groundbreaking shift in scientific methodology. The primary research goals include advancing sustainable steel, designing energy storage salts, developing safe plastic additives, and exploring plant-based proteins for food innovation[47].

The project leverages a multidimensional approach to AI. One technique, pioneered by lvl professor Max Welling, uses graph neural networks to analyse molecular structures as spatial networks. This method enables AI to understand molecular properties by analysing atomic connections in three-dimensional space, similar to the networks that underpin DeepMind's game-playing AI models like AlphaGo. In this way, AI perceives molecules as "networks," with

---

[46] https://www.weforum.org/stories/2024/07/generative-ai-smart-cities/
[47] https://www.uva.nl/en/shared-content/faculteiten/en/faculteit-der-natuurwetenschappen-wiskunde-en-informatica/news/2024/02/shaping-the-future-of-materials-using-artificial-intelligence.html?cb

nodes representing atoms and bonds signifying interactions[47].

Another technique, derived from natural language processing, interprets molecular formulas as a chemical language. Just as AI interprets human words, these models view molecules as chemical phrases, using a "chemical grammar" to forecast interactions. This approach gives AI a remarkable capacity to predict molecular behaviours and properties, vastly expanding the possibilities in sustainable chemistry[48].

With these methods, AI4SMM is positioned to drive sustainable advancements across various domains, from renewable energy solutions to consumer goods. Ensing envisions an Amsterdam-based consortium that could foster long-term partnerships with academic and industry players, aligning perfectly with the city's collaborative and innovative culture[48].

The UvA Faculty of Science has laid the foundation for AI4SMM through a series of two-year postdoctoral projects, bringing together specialists from diverse scientific backgrounds. This early success has already attracted interest from industry, reinforcing Amsterdam's status as a premier hub for AI-driven research in sustainable chemistry.

---

[48] https://www.iamsterdam.com/en/business/uva-developing-ai-powered-innovations-in-sustainable-materials

Ensing sees a growing consortium of PhD students and researchers as vital to AI4SMM's momentum, allowing it to secure substantial funding from European and national grants[48][47].

Dallas: Enhance Self-Driving Trucks

Dallas is rapidly evolving into a pivotal center for the development and implementation of autonomous vehicles (AVs). This transformation is driven by a combination of technological advancements, strategic partnerships, and a supportive regulatory environment. As autonomous vehicles become more integrated into urban transportation systems, Dallas exemplifies both the potential benefits and the challenges associated with this innovative technology.

The city has become a testing ground for various autonomous vehicle applications, particularly in the realms of freight transport and ride-sharing services. Companies such as Aurora Innovation are conducting extensive trials of autonomous trucks in the Dallas-Fort Worth area. Aurora plans to deploy 20 driverless trucks to haul freight along Interstate 45 between Dallas and Houston, marking a significant milestone in autonomous transportation. These trucks are designed to navigate complex urban environments while transporting goods efficiently, utilizing advanced sensors like lidar and radar to ensure safety on the roads[49].

In addition to freight transport, Dallas is also witnessing advancements in autonomous ride-sharing services. Cruise, a self-driving ride-hailing company owned by General Motors, has been actively working to launch its services in the city. However, this initiative faced setbacks due to safety concerns following incidents in other cities, such as San Francisco, where a pedestrian was struck and dragged by one of Cruise's vehicles. In response to these incidents, the California Department of Motor Vehicles ruled that Cruise's autonomous vehicles were "not safe for public operation," leading to a temporary halt in their deployment [50]. As a result, Cruise has opted to initially deploy vehicles with human drivers while it reassesses its safety protocols. This cautious approach highlights the importance of public trust in the deployment of autonomous vehicles.

Despite these challenges, Dallas is not alone in its pursuit of autonomous vehicle technology. Nearby Arlington has successfully implemented its own autonomous ride-sharing program through May Mobility, which has been operational since 2021. This program has

---

[49] https://www.telematicswire.net/aurora-to-deploy-20-driverless-trucks-on-dallas-houston-route/
[50] https://www.cbsnews.com/texas/news/self-driving-car-company-soft-launching-in-dallas/

already transported hundreds of riders daily, showcasing the potential for successful integration of AVs into urban transportation systems[51]. The contrast between Arlington's success and Dallas's cautious approach reflects the varying strategies cities are adopting as they navigate the complexities of introducing autonomous technology.

Boston: The Urban Landscape

In Boston's journey towards a more bicycle-friendly city, planners are taking inspiration from Copenhagen's renowned cycling infrastructure. However, rather than sending residents across the Atlantic to witness these changes firsthand, generative AI is helping Bostonians visualize a transformed urban landscape right at home. Professor Jinhua Zhao from MIT explained that AI technology can virtually overlay Copenhagen's bike infrastructure onto Boston's own streets, offering residents a vivid picture of how their city might look with an extensive bicycle network. This AI-driven visualization allows Bostonians to engage with the proposed changes in a tangible way, encouraging greater acceptance of a more bike-centric city layout[46].

Boston's engagement with generative AI extends beyond urban planning and into governmental reform.

---

[51] https://www.governing.com/policy/north-texas-city-drives-ahead-with-driverless-vehicles

Many U.S. government processes, designed over 150 years ago, have become bureaucratic and rigid. Generative AI offers a chance to break free from these outdated structures, presenting an opportunity to shift public administration towards efficiency and citizen-cantered governance. Generative AI tools, such as OpenAI's ChatGPT, could empower city employees to analyse data, detect patterns, and make decisions more swiftly, reducing the need for repetitive approvals and cutting through red tape[52].

In practice, Boston has already experimented with generative AI by uploading 311 service data, where AI-generated suggestions included time series analysis by case type and neighbourhood-based comparisons. This allowed city officials to focus on identifying discrepancies and service gaps without the need for advanced technical skills. By simplifying data analysis with AI-driven visualizations, such as maps and graphs, generative AI enables city officials from various backgrounds to make data-informed decisions that improve community services[52].

A key component of this AI integration is enabling frontline workers with AI tools to proactively address local issues. Empowering these workers to make decisions directly fosters a more responsive government, where residents' needs can be met efficiently. AI tools also

---

[52]https://www.fastcompany.com/90983427/chatgpt-generative-ai-government-reform-biden-garces-boston-goldsmith-harvard

enhance accountability, allowing both civic leaders and the public to monitor project progress, create visual maps, and establish compliance checklists for ongoing initiatives. This transparency in government operations can build trust with citizens, encouraging community involvement.

However, the transition to AI-powered governance brings challenges. Training public employees in data analysis skills, ensuring privacy, and safeguarding against algorithmic bias are all essential to responsible AI integration. Although Boston faces these obstacles, generative AI's potential to revitalize local government remains promising, offering a model for efficient, citizen-focused governance. Through AI, Boston aims to foster a city that's not only bike-friendly but also a leader in digital-age public administration[52].

Chapter 6

Generative AI: Redefining Global Business

The business industry is experiencing a transformative shift through generative AI. According to McKinsey, the banking industry—alongside high-tech and life sciences—stands to unlock tremendous value from generative AI, with potential gains ranging from $200 billion to $340 billion annually [53]. This groundbreaking technology could transform revenue streams and redefine industry standards, making generative AI a game-changer for financial institutions aiming to stay ahead.

Apple: Integration of Generative AI

Among Fortune 500 companies, Apple exemplifies how generative AI can redefine user experience and productivity. Through its groundbreaking Apple Intelligence system, Apple has seamlessly incorporated generative AI into its core products, including iPhone, iPad, and Mac, setting a new benchmark for what's possible in personal technology[54].

---

[53] https://itrexgroup.com/blog/generative-ai-in banking/#:~:text=According%20to%20McKinsey%20research%2C%20banking,billion%20and%20%24340%20billion%20annually.

[54] https://www.apple.com/sg/newsroom/2024/06/introducing-apple-intelligence-for-iphone-ipad-and-mac/

What makes Apple Intelligence unique is its ability to combine generative models with a user's personal context. This integration enables the system to deliver tailored, actionable insights while maintaining Apple's hallmark commitment to privacy through its Private Cloud Compute framework. By balancing on-device processing with secure, server-based models, Apple provides users with both efficiency and peace of mind—a critical advancement in today's data-conscious era[54].

Apple Intelligence enhances everyday tasks with tools that elevate writing, communication, and organization. Features like Rewrite, which adjusts tone and style, and proofread, which ensures grammar accuracy while offering explanations, empower users to communicate with confidence. For those overwhelmed by information, the Summarize function transforms lengthy emails or documents into concise, actionable summaries. In Mail, Priority Messages highlight the most urgent updates, while Smart Reply generates quick responses, streamlining workflows. Even notifications have been optimized with features like Priority Notifications and Reduce Interruptions, ensuring users stay focused on what truly matter[54].

Apple's use of generative AI demonstrates how innovation can simplify and enrich users' lives while safeguarding their privacy. This approach highlights the potential for generative AI not just to improve technology, but to redefine how businesses engage with their customers.

As we explore other Fortune 500 companies and their use of generative AI, Apple's example offers a clear message: this technology is a catalyst for change, empowering businesses to innovate responsibly while enhancing user experience in unprecedented ways[54].

Starbucks: Revolutionizing Business with AI

Starbucks has long been a trailblazer in redefining customer experiences, and its foray into artificial intelligence demonstrates its unwavering commitment to innovation. Although Starbucks first ventured into AI in 2019 with the introduction of Deep Brew[55], its proprietary platform, the company has significantly amplified its digital transformation in recent years. With the rise of generative AI in the early 2020s, Starbucks seized the opportunity to harness this cutting-edge technology. The announcement of its three-year reinvention plan in September 2023 signalled a bold new chapter, underscoring a strategic focus on automation, AI, and digital personalization to cater to the evolving preferences of younger, tech-savvy consumers[56].

---

[55] https://finance.yahoo.com/news/starbucks-to-use-ai-at-the-drive-thru-151414041.html
[56] https://aiexpert.network/case-study-starbucks-revolutionizes-the-coffee-experience-with-ai/

At the core of Starbucks' transformation lies Deep Brew, an advanced AI platform that serves as the backbone of the company's digital innovation efforts. Leveraging the power of generative AI, Deep Brew drives Starbucks' personalization engine, ensuring tailored customer interactions, from customized marketing messages to menu recommendations. This deep understanding of consumer behaviour allows Starbucks to create meaningful, individualized experiences that foster loyalty. For example, customers might receive a timely app notification offering a discount on their favourite drink or a personalized rewards incentive based on their purchase history, seamlessly integrating technology into their daily lives[56] [57].

Operationally, Deep Brew has proven to be a game-changer. Starbucks has integrated AI across its store network to streamline performance and improve efficiency. AI-powered inventory management systems predict product demand with remarkable accuracy, ensuring that stores remain stocked while minimizing waste. In parallel, AI-driven labor allocation tools optimize staffing, guaranteeing that stores are adequately manned during peak hours without unnecessary overhead. The implementation of smart equipment, such as AI-enabled coffee makers, has further revolutionized store operations

---

[57] https://rickhuckstep.medium.com/how-starbucks-leverages-ai-for-customer-engagement-eee269b489fc

by reducing beverage preparation times, improving consistency, and enhancing overall service quality[56].

The benefits of these AI-driven initiatives are already evident. Starbucks has reported record quarterly earnings and a substantial increase in active membership within its Rewards program, a cornerstone of its personalization strategy[56] above. The program's success is fueled by AI-generated insights that offer targeted rewards, creating compelling incentives for frequent visits and higher spending. This combination of operational excellence and personalized engagement underscores Starbucks' ability to adapt to the digital age while staying true to its mission of delivering exceptional customer experiences.

However, the road to full AI integration has not been without challenges. As a global brand with diverse markets, Starbucks faces the complexity of tailoring AI solutions to varying consumer behaviours and preferences. Implementing new technologies at scale requires significant investment in infrastructure and extensive training for employees to ensure they can effectively work alongside advanced tools. Additionally, the adoption of AI has necessitated a cultural shift within the company, blending technological innovation with Starbucks' traditional emphasis on human connection and quality service[56].

Mastercard: Personalization & Security

Mastercard is leveraging generative AI chatbots to enhance customer service, providing immediate, personalized responses to inquiries such as balance checks and transaction histories. This innovation facilitates seamless customer interactions and improves service efficiency. Additionally, Mastercard employs AI-driven predictive models to detect and prevent fraud by analysing individual behaviours to identify unusual activities that may indicate fraudulent actions. This dual approach not only enhances customer experience but also strengthens security measures, demonstrating that a robust AI strategy can yield significant results without compromising data integrity[58].

Morgan Stanley: Enhancing Financial Advisory

Morgan Stanley's latest generative AI tool, AskResearchGPT, is redefining how Investment Banking, Sales & Trading, and Research teams deliver insights. Imagine having access to over 70,000 proprietary research reports distilled into actionable insights with just a click. AskResearchGPT does precisely that, integrating seamlessly

---

[58] https://www.infosecurity-magazine.com/news/mastercard-fraud-detection/

into everyday workflows to empower teams with a powerful edge in servicing institutional clients[59].

Built on OpenAI's GPT-4, AskResearchGPT goes beyond the traditional AskResearch chatbot by synthesizing data to answer complex, multi-layered questions. Staff can quickly navigate Morgan Stanley's extensive research library, allowing them to provide richer, deeper analyses that drive smarter decisions and better outcomes[59].

To make this even more practical, AskResearchGPT integrates a patented one-click workflow, where findings can be automatically transferred into email drafts, ready for customization and client-sharing. Embedded hyperlinks connect users directly to original research, so teams and clients can dive deeper when needed, enhancing transparency and client trust[59].

Allstate & BCG: Better Customer Experience

Allstate, one of the largest property and liability insurers in the U.S. and a Forbes 100 company, has partnered with Boston Consulting Group (BCG) to take CX to a new level using Gen AI. This partnership taps into the expertise of BCG X, BCG's dedicated tech-build division, and

---

[59] https://www.morganstanley.com/press-releases/morgan-stanley-research-announces-askresearchgpt

aims to revolutionize Allstate's customer interactions by harnessing the capabilities of advanced predictive modelling and AI insights. The goal? To proactively identify and address customer needs before they even become issues[60].

For Allstate and BCG, this technology holds the potential to improve CX across multiple areas, with a particular focus on issue resolution. By using predictive models, Allstate can gain valuable insights into customer behaviour, helping agents respond faster and with greater accuracy. This AI-powered approach triples the predictive performance of previous models, allowing Allstate to quickly identify customer journeys that need special attention[60].

The success of Allstate's AI initiative reflects the strength of its collaboration with BCG. Together, they have tested and refined a model that not only identifies customer needs but does so faster and with greater precision. By combining existing customer data with insights from generative AI, the model continually improves, creating a dynamic, responsive system. This model frees Allstate's human employees to handle more complex cases while streamlining routine interactions, enhancing the customer journey from start to finish. customer experience[60].

---

[60] https://insurtechdigital.com/technology-and-ai/allstate-bcg-partner-harnesses-gen-ai-to-transform-cx

Goldman Sachs: Unified Power and Precision

Goldman Sachs has adopted a centralized AI strategy, consolidating all AI initiatives under its GS AI Platform—a secure, unified hub that drives AI innovation while maintaining rigorous compliance standards. This platform leverages partnerships with tech leaders like Microsoft and Google, integrating advanced models such as OpenAI's GPT-3.5 and GPT-4, Google's Gemini, and Meta's Llama. With this multi-model flexibility, Goldman Sachs can deliver tailored, high-impact AI solutions that address a range of business needs[61].

The first deployment focuses on code generation—a prime application for generative AI. By using GitHub Copilot, Goldman Sachs aims to empower developers to boost productivity by up to 20%, reducing development timelines from months to just weeks. This tool goes beyond speed; it enhances precision, enabling developers to produce high-quality code faster than ever[61].

The platform's impact extends further. Selected employees have direct access to develop customized applications, including an AI-powered copilot for investment bankers, which swiftly mines an extensive archive of public and proprietary documents to deliver

---

[61] https://aiexpert.network/goldman-sachs-ai/

insights within seconds. For Goldman Sachs, this real-time, data-rich intelligence drives decision-making that keeps the firm ahead of the curve[61].

Goldman Sachs' AI strategy carefully balances innovation with rigorous security and compliance. The GS AI Platform incorporates robust safety protocols, ensuring that each application strictly adheres to regulatory standards. This centralized, secure approach enables Goldman Sachs to expand AI use while upholding client trust and data integrity[61].

Klarna: Reinventing Shopping

Klarna, the global AI-powered payments network and shopping assistant, is on a mission to transform shopping and payment experiences for millions. When ChatGPT launched in 2022, Klarna Co-founder and CEO Sebastian Siemiatkowski immediately saw the opportunity. Klarna quickly became the first European company—and the first fintech worldwide—to launch a ChatGPT plugin, pioneering a new era of AI-driven customer engagement.

Imagine effortlessly asking an AI tool for the perfect pair of sneakers under $150 and receiving curated options instantly. That's the vision behind Klarna's ChatGPT plugin. ChatGPT connects users to Klarna's search-and-compare tool, allowing shoppers to discover the best prices and products in a matter of moments—turning online shopping into a smooth, personalized journey[62].

Klarna's AI assistant, powered by OpenAI, supports 150 million users worldwide with everything from multilingual customer service to refund management. The impact in just one month has been remarkable. In just its first month live, Klarna's AI assistant has delivered game-changing results[62]:

- 2.3 million conversations handled—covering two-thirds of all customer service chats.
- Equivalent to 700 full-time agents' work, demonstrating unparalleled efficiency.
- Matching human satisfaction scores while maintaining high-quality customer interactions.
- 25% reduction in repeat inquiries, thanks to greater accuracy in resolving issues.
- Response time slashed to under 2 minutes per interaction, down from 11 minutes.
- Available 24/7 across 23 markets and over 35 languages, providing round-the-clock support.
- Projected to boost profits by $40 million in 2024, underscoring AI's transformative impact.
- Klarna's AI assistant is more than a tool; it's a revolution in customer service that's setting new standards for speed, accuracy, and satisfaction worldwide[62].

Furthermore, Klarna's adoption of ChatGPT extends to its entire workforce. With 90% of employees using generative AI daily, the technology is empowering teams across Communications, Marketing, Legal, and beyond. The company claimed that this AI revolution means superior experiences for customers, exciting challenges for our teams, and strong returns for investors[62].

Microsoft: Engagement Redefined with Copilot

Microsoft's approach leverages generative AI across its ecosystem to make everyday life and work more personal and engaging. Microsoft Copilot, the AI-powered companion, plays a pivotal role in this shift. With a doubling of conversations year-on-year, consumer journeys that combine Microsoft Copilot with traditional search have grown by 85%, while mobile usage has increased over 2.5x, illustrating Copilot's impact on how users interact with content[63].

Since its launch in 2023, Microsoft Copilot has pioneered a new approach to digital advertising, integrating ads across search and product experiences. This platform is transforming engagement, driving 69% stronger click-

---

[62] https://openai.com/index/klarna/
[63] https://about.ads.microsoft.com/en/blog/post/october-2024/transforming-audience-engagement-with-generative-ai

through rates and 76% higher conversion rates on lower-funnel ads compared to traditional search. Ad formats, including Vertical ads, Multimedia ads, and Product ads, benefit from Copilot's targeted and context-aware approach[63].

Microsoft Copilot's latest evolution redefines user-cantered advertising. In this new experience, organic and sponsored content are distinct yet seamlessly integrated, enhancing both relevance and usefulness. Ads are positioned within a streamlined layout beneath Copilot's responses, with an emphasis on context-specific relevance[63].

The "ad voice" feature introduces ads in a conversational manner, connecting them directly to the user's journey. This approach means that ad blocks appear only when Copilot recognizes how they naturally tie into the user's conversation, creating a more intuitive and engaging experience.

This enhanced ad experience is already rolling out on copilot.microsoft.com, with expansion planned across Microsoft's mobile apps and platforms like Bing and Edge. Bing's generative search feature, now live since October 1, further enhances engagement by generating curated, context-rich responses.

Looking ahead, Microsoft envisions an even deeper level of personalization through immersive, interactive ads that adapt to each user's context and needs. The goal is to enable brands to create their own "brand voices," allowing Copilot to offer exclusive deals, product details, and trusted recommendations in relevant conversations, enhancing both user experience and brand engagement[63].

Microsoft's vision extends to making AI a powerful tool for advertisers. Copilot in the Microsoft Advertising Platform boosts productivity and creativity, helping marketers unlock insights and optimize performance. Over the past year, Copilot has allowed users to refine marketing messages, generate diverse creative assets, and drive more targeted personalization[63].

Adobe: Enhancing Creative Tools

Adobe has integrated generative AI across its suite of products to enhance the tools used by designers, content creators, and professionals managing complex documents. Generative AI is a form of artificial intelligence that learns from existing data to create new content, whether it be images, text, or other forms of media. Adobe's approach to this technology aims to streamline the user experience by embedding AI capabilities directly within familiar workflows[64].

---

[64] https://helpx.adobe.com/creative-cloud/generative-ai-overview.html

Firefly is Adobe's family of generative AI models, designed specifically to work within the Adobe ecosystem. It enables users to generate content, such as images or text effects, based on straightforward prompts. Firefly's integration allows users to experiment and iterate quickly without leaving the Adobe applications they're accustomed to. This feature is particularly valuable for exploring new ideas, as users can generate visuals that respond to specific prompts, facilitating a more intuitive and efficient creative process[64].

In Adobe Acrobat, generative AI functions help users sift through large volumes of text-based data. With features like Generative Summary (Beta) and an AI-powered Assistant, Acrobat users can extract key insights from lengthy PDFs, generate summaries, and find specific information with ease. The Assistant also offers suggested questions to guide further exploration within documents, making information retrieval faster and more accessible[64].

Adobe's use of generative AI highlights how such technology can be applied practically in both creative and analytical contexts. For design, Firefly supports a fast, responsive process that aids in visualization and experimentation. In document management, Acrobat's AI tools save time and reduce manual effort, shifting the focus toward interpreting information rather than simply locating it. Adobe's integration of generative AI exemplifies how companies are moving beyond traditional AI applications to create more interactive, adaptive experiences[64].

Salesforce: Redefining Customer Relations

Imagine a CRM that doesn't just store information but actively shapes interactions, adapting in real-time to create meaningful, personalized experiences. This is the vision Salesforce brings to life with Einstein GPT—the first generative AI built exclusively for CRM. Announced in March 2023, Einstein GPT combines generative AI's creative power with Salesforce's extensive data ecosystem, allowing companies to interact with customers in ways that are more insightful, dynamic, and uniquely personalized.

Einstein GPT operates seamlessly across Salesforce's core functions, making it a versatile tool for transforming the everyday tasks of sales, marketing, customer service, and even development[65].

Here's how it changes the game:
- Sales: Imagine sales emails that write themselves, tailored to the customer's latest interactions. Einstein GPT automates sales tasks like composing emails, scheduling follow-ups, and preparing for meetings, allowing teams to focus on building relationships rather than drafting responses[65].

---

[65]https://www.salesforce.com/news/pressreleases/2023/03/07/einstein-generative-ai/

- Customer Service: Einstein GPT empowers support agents to respond faster and with greater accuracy by generating replies based on past cases, creating a more empathetic and effective customer experience[65].
- Marketing: With Einstein GPT, marketing campaigns become adaptive and targeted, delivering content tailored to each customer's needs across email, mobile, and web channels.
- In Slack: Integrated with OpenAI's ChatGPT, Einstein GPT for Slack can summarize conversations, answer questions, and even provide draft responses, making Slack a more powerful tool for collaboration[65].
- For Developers: Salesforce developers can now generate code, troubleshoot faster, and streamline complex tasks with Einstein GPT, allowing for faster, more efficient development within the Salesforce platform[65].

Einstein GPT's unique strength lies in its ability to draw from Salesforce's Data Cloud, which unifies real-time customer data. This means that the AI-generated content isn't static; it continuously adapts to the latest customer information, providing relevant responses that evolve as customer needs change. This flexibility makes Einstein GPT an invaluable tool for businesses aiming to provide responsive, intelligent service[65].

Salesforce's vision for generative AI goes beyond immediate applications. Through Salesforce Ventures, the company has launched a $250 million Generative AI Fund to support startups and drive responsible AI development. This investment reflects Salesforce's commitment to fostering innovation within the generative AI ecosystem, with an eye on building technology that is as ethical as it is effective[65].

In partnership with OpenAI, Salesforce is bridging the gap between traditional CRM and cutting-edge AI. With Einstein GPT, users benefit from the robustness of OpenAI's ChatGPT integrated into the Salesforce platform, expanding the possibilities of what AI can do for CRM. Einstein GPT represents a new era in CRM, where AI actively enhances customer interactions and team productivity. By harnessing generative AI's adaptability and insight, Salesforce offers businesses a smarter, more responsive way to engage customers, empowering them to connect more deeply and effectively than ever before[65].

Chapter 7

What is the Next Big Things After Generative AI?

As Generative AI continues to redefine industries with its ability to create new content and simulate human-like interactions, the next frontier in artificial intelligence is beginning to take shape. The advancements poised to follow Generative AI—Predictive AI, Interactive AI, and Autonomous AI—promise to revolutionize how AI improves accuracy, enhances user interaction, and makes independent decisions. Among these, Predictive AI stands out as a transformative force, leveraging data to anticipate outcomes and enable proactive strategies across various domains.

Predictive AI

Predictive AI focuses on identifying patterns and forecasting future events using statistical analysis and machine learning. By analysing vast amounts of historical data, this branch of AI offers organizations the ability to anticipate customer behaviour, market trends, and potential risks. Unlike descriptive analytics, which explains past occurrences, or prescriptive analytics, which suggests actions to achieve specific outcomes, Predictive AI excels in forecasting what is likely to happen, helping businesses make informed decisions with confidence.

At the core of Predictive AI lies its reliance on high-quality data and sophisticated algorithms. Data preparation is a critical first step, where information from diverse sources is collected, cleaned, and validated to eliminate inconsistencies or biases. Once prepared, the data is fed into advanced machine learning models, such as neural networks, decision trees, or regression models, which iteratively learn and refine their predictions. The accuracy of these models improves as they process larger datasets over time, identifying intricate patterns and relationships that might elude human analysts.

Embeddings, a specialized technique used in predictive AI, play a crucial role in making predictions more precise. By transforming data into mathematical vectors and clustering similar information together, embeddings enable AI to analyse vast datasets efficiently, drawing connections and insights that drive accurate forecasts. This process, combined with big data analytics, ensures that predictive models remain reliable and relevant, even as the volume and complexity of data grow.

The applications of Predictive AI span numerous industries and are reshaping traditional processes. In healthcare, predictive models can forecast potential medical conditions based on a patient's history, enabling early intervention and personalized care. In finance, Predictive AI assists in analysing transaction data to detect fraud or anticipate market trends for better investment strategies. Retail and e-commerce businesses leverage predictive insights to optimize inventory management, forecast consumer demand, and refine pricing strategies. Supply chain management benefits from Predictive AI's ability to anticipate disruptions, such as traffic congestion, allowing companies to enhance logistics and delivery efficiency.

Predictive maintenance is another area where this technology shines, using data from machinery sensors to identify potential failures before they occur, minimizing downtime and reducing costs. Streaming platforms and online retailers employ predictive recommendation systems to enhance user experiences by suggesting content or products tailored to individual preferences. The potential for Predictive AI to free up employees' time by automating data analysis further underscores its value, allowing human workers to focus on creativity and decision-making.

While Predictive AI and Generative AI serve different purposes, they often complement each other. Predictive AI focuses on forecasting outcomes and guiding decisions, while Generative AI creates new content, such as text, images, or music, based on user prompts. Together, these technologies empower businesses to enhance efficiency, innovation, and customer engagement. For example, a company could use Predictive AI to identify customer preferences and Generative AI to create personalized marketing content.

However, the widespread adoption of Predictive AI raises important considerations. Ethical concerns, such as the risk of biases in data or algorithms, must be addressed to ensure fair and trustworthy outcomes. Transparency and explainability are crucial, especially in sensitive sectors like healthcare and finance, where understanding how predictions are made is essential for building trust and maintaining compliance with regulations.

Integrating Predictive AI into existing workflows is vital for organizations to unlock its full potential. Predictions must be actionable and aligned with strategic goals, ensuring that AI insights translate into meaningful business improvements. While Predictive AI enables more precise decision-making, human judgment remains indispensable, particularly when navigating uncertainties or ethical dilemmas.

The evolution from Generative AI to Predictive AI marks a significant milestone in artificial intelligence. By enabling businesses to anticipate and prepare for the future, Predictive AI sets the stage for even more advanced developments, such as Interactive AI and Autonomous AI. As we move toward a future defined by greater automation and intelligence, Predictive AI is not just the next big thing—it is a cornerstone for shaping a smarter, more proactive world.

Interactive AI

Interactive Artificial Intelligence (AI) is rapidly becoming a transformative force in the AI landscape, bridging the gap between static data processing and dynamic, two-way engagement. Unlike traditional AI, which relies on predefined algorithms to analyse data and make decisions, interactive AI thrives on real-time communication. It enables systems to respond dynamically to user inputs, creating a seamless and engaging experience. This chapter explores the essence of interactive AI, its diverse applications, and its potential to revolutionize industries and everyday interactions.

Interactive AI systems are designed to understand and respond to natural language, fostering a conversational interface that mimics human interaction. This capability is made possible by advances in natural language processing (NLP), which allow AI to comprehend, interpret, and generate human language effectively. Through NLP, interactive AI can analyse user queries, extract contextual meaning, and generate personalized responses, making interactions more intuitive and satisfying.

The applications of interactive AI span a wide range of industries, with notable use cases in customer service, virtual assistants, and e-commerce. In customer service, chatbots powered by interactive AI provide instant, personalized assistance, addressing customer inquiries and resolving issues efficiently. Virtual assistants like Alexa and Google Assistant rely on interactive AI to perform tasks, answer questions, and adapt to user preferences, delivering a tailored and user-centric experience. On e-commerce platforms, interactive AI enhances the shopping journey by offering personalized product recommendations, guiding customers through the purchase process, and providing support at every stage.

Interactive AI's ability to deliver real-time and personalized experiences has a profound impact on user engagement. By understanding the context and preferences of users, interactive AI streamlines process and creates meaningful interactions that build trust and satisfaction. In digital marketing, for instance, interactive AI enables dynamic content creation, automated lead nurturing, and precise targeting based on user behaviour. This results in more effective campaigns, higher engagement, and improved conversion rates. Similarly, on social media platforms, interactive AI facilitates personalized messaging, interactive polls, and real-time responses, driving deeper connections between brands and their audiences.

Educational technology is another domain where interactive AI is making significant strides. By offering adaptive learning experiences, real-time feedback, and interactive exercises, it caters to diverse learning styles and fosters greater student engagement. This personalized approach has the potential to enhance educational outcomes and democratize access to quality learning resources.

Despite its vast potential, implementing interactive AI presents certain challenges. Ensuring the accuracy and relevance of AI responses is critical, as errors in understanding user input can undermine trust. Ethical considerations, including transparency, data privacy, and bias mitigation, must also be addressed. Developers must prioritize building systems that are not only effective but also responsible and aligned with user interests.

Interactive AI's benefits far outweigh its limitations, making it a vital tool for businesses looking to enhance customer experience and streamline operations. By automating routine tasks, interactive AI frees employees to focus on creative and strategic responsibilities, driving productivity and innovation. Moreover, its role in content personalization, from tailored email marketing campaigns to customized recommendations on websites and mobile apps, underscores its versatility and impact on modern business strategies.

As we look to the future, interactive AI is set to shape remote work environments, enabling real-time language translation, automated meeting summaries, and personalized task management. These capabilities promise to enhance productivity and foster collaboration across global teams. However, the ethical development of interactive AI requires robust frameworks that ensure accountability, transparency, and user privacy. Developers must remain vigilant against perpetuating biases and infringing on individual rights, striving to create systems that prioritize fairness and inclusivity.

Interactive AI represents a significant evolution in artificial intelligence, moving beyond static computation to create dynamic, human-like interactions. Its ability to adapt, personalize, and engage positions it as a cornerstone of the next wave of AI innovation. By harnessing its potential responsibly, businesses and developers can unlock new possibilities, transforming industries and enriching human experiences in the digital age.

Autonomous AI

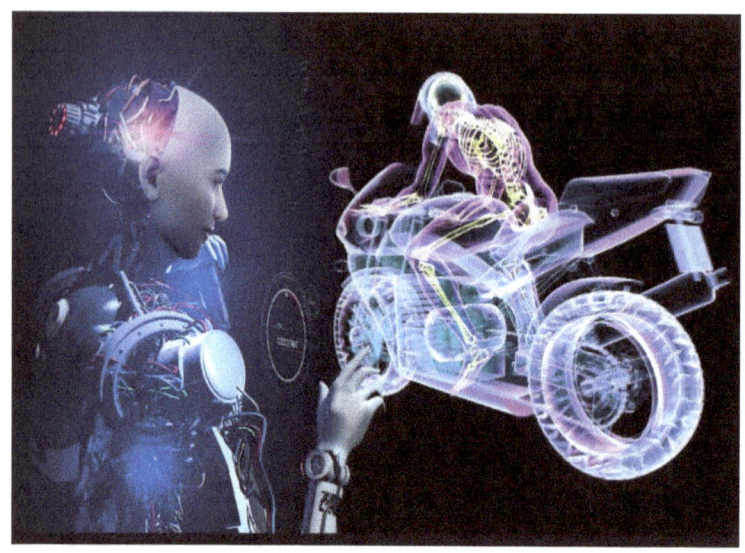

Autonomous Artificial Intelligence (AI) is not just a technological advancement—it's a revolution. Imagine a world where machines learn, adapt, and act on their own, creating seamless solutions for the problems we didn't even know we had. Self-driving cars navigate the most complex roads without a hitch, smart homes anticipate your needs before you voice them, and software tools handle your daily tasks while you focus on what truly matters. Autonomous AI is no longer a futuristic dream; it's the here and now, steadily transforming the way we live, work, and innovate.

What makes autonomous AI truly remarkable is its ability to operate independently. Unlike traditional AI, which often relies on human input to function, autonomous

AI thrives on its capacity to gather data, analyse it, and make decisions without intervention. It uses sensors to observe the world, algorithms to process data, and a structured framework to achieve goals autonomously. These systems don't just follow instructions—they create pathways to success, adapting and improving over time.

This capability is more than a technological breakthrough; it's an enabler of efficiency, accuracy, and personalization. Businesses can now automate mundane tasks, freeing up time and resources for innovation. Smart factories increase production capacity while reducing errors. Marketing campaigns are powered by algorithms that deliver hyper-personalized recommendations, captivating customers like never before. Whether it's healthcare diagnostics, logistics optimization, or education, autonomous AI is rewriting the rules and showing us what's possible when intelligence meets independence.

However, like any great innovation, it comes with challenges. Autonomous AI raises questions about ethics, fairness, and data security. Who is accountable if a system makes a flawed decision? How do we ensure that algorithms don't reinforce bias or inequality? And how can we protect sensitive data from misuse? These are not trivial concerns. They demand thoughtful regulation, ethical oversight, and a shared commitment to responsible innovation.

Yet the promise of autonomous AI far outweighs its challenges. As we step further into the age of automation, this technology offers a profound opportunity to redefine how we work and live. It's not just about creating smarter machines—it's about creating a smarter society.

AI Your Future- Embrace the Transformation

As we look toward the future, one thing is clear: AI is evolving rapidly. While traditional AI has transformed industries by solving specific challenges, the new era of AI introduces adaptability, creativity, and human-like understanding. It doesn't just automate tasks—it reimagines them, opening doors to innovations that could possibly reshape our lives and industries.

The new era of AI is not confined to rigid systems or predefined algorithms. Instead, it leverages advanced models capable of understanding context, learning dynamically, and creating personalized, intelligent solutions. Industries that once relied on traditional AI are now discovering how this modern technology could possibly unlock even greater potential.

Consider these comparisons:

- Healthcare breakthroughs: Traditional AI accelerated Johnson & Johnson's vaccine development [66]. The new era of AI could possibly integrate real-time health data, provide multilingual patient support, and personalize treatment plans using genetic insights.

---

[66] https://www.jnj.com/innovation/artificial-intelligence-in-healthcare

- Retail innovations: McDonald's use AI to streamline operations[67]. The new era of AI could possible deliver hyper-personalized recommendations, real-time customer sentiment analysis, and even predictive forecasts for global demand.

- Entertainment excellence: Netflix's traditional AI personalizes watchlists[68]. The new era of AI could possibly enable viewers to co-create interactive content, dynamically generate summaries, or customize story endings in real-time.

- Smart cities: Traditional AI optimizes traffic in London[69]. The new era of AI could possibly provide predictive planning, adjusting city layouts based on evolving trends, and enhance public engagement through conversational tools.

---

[67] https://procureconsupplychain.wbresearch.com/blog/mcdonalds-ai-data-optimize-supply-chain
[68] https://stratoflow.com/how-netflix-recommendation-system-works/
[69] https://www.cow-shed.com/blog/using-artificial-intelligence-to-improve-transport-in-london

- Sustainability advancements: Traditional AI powers Sweden's energy systems[70]. The new era of AI could possibly recommend live energy-saving measures for households, adapt renewable energy production in real time, and automate sustainability reports for governments.

These examples show how the new era of AI is fundamentally different—it's not just smarter, it's more flexible and capable of delivering breakthroughs that traditional AI systems couldn't achieve.

As the possibilities of the new era of AI continue to unfold, success lies in more than adopting new technology—it's about transforming potential into actionable impact. Imagine using AI not just to optimize processes, but to innovate, inspire, and achieve results that truly set you apart.

This journey requires more than tools; it calls for expertise, strategic vision, and a clear understanding of how to harness AI for your unique goals. Whether it's refining strategies, automating workflows, or empowering teams with cutting-edge knowledge, the right guidance can turn challenges into opportunities.

---

[70] https://www.ai.se/en/news/building-better-energy-system-ai

Follow me today for insights, tailored strategies, and a deeper exploration of how AI training, consultation, automation, and coaching can elevate your ambitions. Together, let's unlock the transformative power of AI and create a future where technology works seamlessly to fuel your success.

"AI Your Future!"
—Dr. Koay, Founder and CEO, DKAI Training and Consultancy

www.ingramcontent.com/pod-product-compliance
Lightning Source LLC
Chambersburg PA
CBHW071652240526
45469CB00021B/2269